The American C

Books on the Civil War Era

*Steven E. Woodworth, Associate Professor of History,
Texas Christian University*
SERIES EDITOR

~ The Civil War was the crisis of the Republic's first century —the test, in Abraham Lincoln's words, of whether any free government could long endure. It touched with fire the hearts of a generation, and its story has fired the imaginations of every generation since. This series offers to students of the Civil War, either those continuing or those just beginning their exciting journey into the past, concise overviews of important persons, events, and themes in that remarkable period of America's history.

Volumes Published

James L. Abrahamson. *The Men of Secession and Civil War, 1859–1861* (2000). Cloth ISBN 0-8420-2818-8 Paper ISBN 0-8420-2819-6

Robert G. Tanner. *Retreat to Victory? Confederate Strategy Reconsidered* (2001). Cloth ISBN 0-8420-2881-1 Paper ISBN 0-8420-2882-X

Stephen Davis. *Atlanta Will Fall: Sherman, Joe Johnston, and the Yankee Heavy Battalions* (2001). Cloth ISBN 0-8420-2787-4 Paper ISBN 0-8420-2788-2

Paul Ashdown and Edward Caudill. *The Mosby Myth: A Confederate Hero in Life and Legend* (2002). Cloth ISBN 0-8420-2928-1 Paper ISBN 0-8420-2929-X

Spencer C. Tucker. *A Short History of the Civil War at Sea* (2002). Cloth ISBN 0-8420-2867-6   Paper ISBN 0-8420-2868-4

Richard Bruce Winders. *Crisis in the Southwest: The United States, Mexico, and the Struggle over Texas* (2002). Cloth ISBN 0-8420-2800-5   Paper ISBN 0-8420-2801-3

Ethan S. Rafuse. *A Single Grand Victory: The First Campaign and Battle of Manassas* (2002). Cloth ISBN 0-8420-2875-7 Paper ISBN 0-8420-2876-5

John G. Selby. *Virginians at War: The Civil War Experiences of Seven Young Confederates* (2002). Cloth ISBN 0-8420-5054-X Paper ISBN 0-8420-5055-8

Edward K. Spann. *Gotham at War: New York City, 1860–1865* (2002). Cloth ISBN 0-8420-5056-6   Paper ISBN 0-8420-5057-4

Anne J. Bailey. *War and Ruin: William T. Sherman and the Savannah Campaign* (2002). Cloth ISBN 0-8420-2850-1 Paper ISBN 0-8420-2851-X

Gary Dillard Joiner. *One Damn Blunder from Beginning to End: The Red River Campaign of 1864* (2003). Cloth ISBN 0-8420-2936-2 Paper ISBN 0-8420-2937-0

Steven E. Woodworth. *Beneath a Northern Sky: A Short History of the Gettysburg Campaign* (2003). Cloth ISBN 0-8420-2932-X Paper ISBN 0-8420-2933-8

John C. Waugh. *On the Brink of Civil War: The Compromise of 1850 and How It Changed the Course of American History* (2003). Cloth ISBN 0-8420-2944-3   Paper ISBN 0-8420-2945-1

Eric H. Walther. *The Shattering of the Union: America in the 1850s* (2004). Cloth ISBN 0-8420-2798-X   Paper ISBN 0-8420-2799-8

Mark Thornton and Robert B. Ekelund Jr. *Tariffs, Blockades, and Inflation: The Economics of the Civil War* (2004). Cloth ISBN 0-8420-2960-5   Paper ISBN 0-8420-2961-3

Paul Ashdown and Edward Caudill. *The Myth of Nathan Bedford Forrest* (2004). Cloth ISBN 0-8420-5066-3 Paper ISBN 0-8420-5067-1

Michael B. Ballard. *U. S. Grant: The Making of a General, 1861–1863* (2004). Cloth ISBN 0-8420-2934-6   Paper ISBN 0-8420-2935-4

Tariffs, Blockades, and Inflation

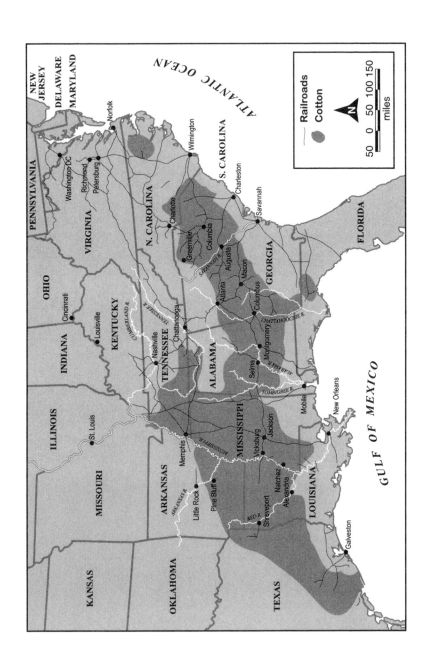

NEW JERSEY

DELAWARE

MARYLAND

ATLANTIC OCEAN

PENNSYLVANIA

VIRGINIA

OHIO

N. CAROLINA

S. CAROLINA

FLORIDA

INDIANA

KENTUCKY

TENNESSEE

GEORGIA

ILLINOIS

ALABAMA

MISSOURI

ARKANSAS

MISSISSIPPI

LOUISIANA

GULF OF MEXICO

KANSAS

OKLAHOMA

TEXAS

Norfolk

Washington DC

Richmond

Petersburg

Wilmington

Charleston

Savannah

Charlotte

Greenville

Columbia

Augusta

Macon

Cincinnati

Louisville

Atlanta

Columbus

Nashville

Chattanooga

Montgomery

Selma

SAVANNAH R.

CHATTAHOOCHEE R.

ALABAMA R.

CUMBERLAND R.

TENNESSEE R.

TOMBIGBEE R.

Mobile

New Orleans

St. Louis

Memphis

Jackson

Vicksburg

MISSISSIPPI R.

Natchez

Alexandria

ARKANSAS R.

Little Rock

Pine Bluff

Shreveport

RED R.

Galveston

Railroads

Cotton

N

miles

50   0   50 100 150

Tariffs, Blockades, and Inflation
The Economics of the Civil War

The American Crisis Series
Books on the Civil War Era
NO. 15

Mark Thornton
and
Robert B. Ekelund Jr.

A Scholarly Resources Inc. Imprint
Wilmington, Delaware

Scholarly Resources Inc.
104 Greenhill Avenue
Wilmington, DE 19805-1897
www.scholarly.com

Library of Congress Cataloging-in-Publication Data

Thornton, Mark.
Tariffs, blockades, and inflation : the economics of the Civil War
/ Mark Thornton and Robert B. Ekelund Jr.
p. cm. — (The American crisis series ; no. 15)
Includes bibliographical references and index.
ISBN 0-8420-2960-5 (alk. paper) — ISBN 0-8420-2961-3 (pbk. :
alk. paper)
1. United States—History—Civil War, 1861–1865—Economic
aspects. I. Ekelund, Robert B. (Robert Burton), 1940–   II. Title.
III. Series.
HC105.6 .T48 2004
973.7'1—dc21

2003014564

To the memory of
David Saurman, a superior economist
and teacher and the best friend
in the world

ABOUT THE AUTHORS

Mark Thornton received his Ph.D. in economics from Auburn University. He has contributed many articles to academic journals and books and is the author of *The Economics of Prohibition* (1991). He has served as the Assistant Superintendent of Banking in Alabama and has taught economics at Auburn University and Columbus State University. Currently he is a Senior Fellow at the Ludwig von Mises Institute and Book Review Editor of the *Quarterly Journal of Austrian Economics*.

Robert B. Ekelund Jr. received his Ph.D. in economics from Louisiana State University. He has contributed many articles to leading academic journals. The coauthor of numerous books including *Secret Origins of Microeconomics: Dupuit and the Engineers* (1999), *Politicized Economies: Monarchy, Monopoly, and Mercantilism* (1997), *Sacred Trust: The Medieval Church as Economic Firm* (1996), and *A History of Economic Theory and Method* (1996), he was the editor of *The Foundations of Regulatory Economics* (1998). He is currently the Edward K. and Catherine L. Lowder Eminent Scholar at Auburn University and Vernon F. Taylor Visiting Distinguished Professor at Trinity University in San Antonio, Texas.

The authors have collaborated on articles on the American Civil War era in *Social Science Quarterly*, *Atlantic Economic Journal*, *Quarterly Journal of Austrian Economics*, *Eastern Economic Journal*, and *International Review of Economics and Business*.

ACKNOWLEDGMENTS

The authors would like to thank their respective institutions (Ludwig von Mises Institute, Columbus State University, Auburn University, and Trinity University) for financial and institutional support of this book. Over the last decade of research and writing, numerous colleagues, coauthors, editors, and referees have helped us craft our ideas concerning an economic understanding of the American Civil War and have contributed directly to improving this manuscript. In particular we would like to thank Mary Jane Roper, Oscar and Joyce Ekelund, Macy Finck, and John Sophocleus for their input and encouragement. In addition, we would like to thank Matthew Hershey at Scholarly Resources as well as the Series Editor, Steven Woodworth.

CONTENTS

INTRODUCTION
How Economics Illuminates the Civil War

Cry "Havoc!" and let slip the dogs of war.
—William Shakespeare, *Julius Caesar*

War and revolution never produce what is wanted but
only some mixture of the old evils with the new ones.
—William G. Sumner, *War* (1903)

DOES DEMOCRACY DEPEND, as a cynic once put it, on deciding never
to vote on something that really matters? If something really
matters, or so the story goes, people are willing to fight over the
issue. Democracies, and other forms of government, do not handle
such internal conflicts very well, but some survive to become
stronger and fundamentally different countries. The United States
of America was one such country. The U.S. Civil War (a topic on
which more books appear every year than on any other in American history) was a watershed in our nation's development. Institutions and the national psyche were altered forever. We are
alternatively horrified and fascinated by the events that took place
between 1861 and 1865, and we seek to understand their causes
and consequences.

Some of the reasons for our fascination with the Civil War are
personal. Many of us had ancestors, from North or South, who
fought, died, or were profoundly affected mentally and physi-
cally by the conflict. More generally, however, the war created
sea changes in the very substance and concept of the American
nation. The directions of these changes were many. Ideologically,
a long and critical debate had raged from the very beginnings of
our country on the nature of the system of political economy. On
the one hand, Alexander Hamilton (and others) supported a
strong federal government as opposed to the looser confederation of states that existed under the Articles of Confederation.
On the other hand, Founding Fathers such as Thomas Jefferson

espoused a limited federal government with most powers reserved to the states. This philosophical and ideological conflict
spilled over into the actual social and political history of the
United States before the Civil War, but much of the controversy
was economic in nature.

The monetary system was a critical case in point, the issue
being whether the banking system should come under the control of the federal government or submit to individual state regulation and market forces. The tension was palpable in the new
nation. The U.S. Constitution prevented any state from establish-
ing its own inflationary banks, and the two attempts to organize
a national bank with special privileges both ended in failure. This
earlier debate was a primary conflict between the Hamiltonians,
who agitated for a national banking system, and the Jeffersonians,
who distrusted banks and paper money altogether. The Civil War
and the monetary crisis that it precipitated resulted in critical
changes in money and banking institutions. In 1863, in the midst
of the war, the National Banking Act imposed federal controls
over the banking system. While the Banking Act did not solve
the so-called problems of the U.S. monetary system (critics claim
that it created more than it solved), it was the beginning of the
government's management that led to the Federal Reserve Act
passed by Congress early in the twentieth century (1913).

The Civil War also marked a watershed in the states' rights
controversy. As suggested by the ideological conflicts mentioned
above, issues relating to states' rights versus those exercised by
the federal government were paramount. Whether slavery, a
prominent institution in the South, could be extended to new areas of the expanding country was a principal political issue. But
of high importance, North and South, was the matter of the tariff. Tariffs on international trade served two purposes: to finance
the federal government and to protect domestic manufacturers
and their employees from foreign competition. In general, Northern manufacturing interests benefited from high tariffs, Southerners from low tariffs. Ultimately, the tensions raised by this issue
were important in bringing the country to war and to constitutional amendments that curtailed states' rights.

These comments suggest that economics is necessary to understand the causes, course, and consequences of the Civil War.

Indeed, economics is a means of explaining and understanding history and all history is written with some theoretical structure, whether good or bad, implicit or explicit. The many excellent and varied historical studies appearing on the Civil War, from the multiplicity of new books to television specials, are not only entertaining but can be enormously valuable in understanding the war when grounded in good theory. The economic history of the factors leading to war—those pertaining to both its conduct and its aftermath—demonstrates the power of modern economic analysis to provide critical insights into this seminal U.S. conflict.

Important caveats concerning our treatment of economic aspects of the war must be made at the outset. The gross immorality of slavery is now the central explanation for the Civil War, and it was unquestionably interwoven into the moral, ideological, political, and economic causes of the conflict. Economists, however, might refer to slavery as a necessary but not a sufficient cause because other factors were required to precipitate the war at the particular time when it began. So much has been written by economists and historians on this critical issue, however, that we largely, but not completely, eschew the matter, focusing instead on the issues of tariffs, the blockade, and inflation. Thus our work is not about the economics of slavery. Further, inasmuch as the specific relative importance of economic cause and effect cannot ever be determined with accuracy at such a distance, we make no specific numerical claims for one economic element versus another or for economic elements versus moral ones in our study of causes. In short, the moral centrality of the slavery issue in bringing about the war is not in debate here because it is difficult for economists to ascribe motives that would lead to this war. Did Southerners defend states' rights to protect slavery or to guard against federal economic controls? Did Northerners oppose slavery on moral and religious grounds or from the perception of possible economic and political gains? The discovery of motives is the purview of in-depth historical research and historical biography.

In recent years it has generally been conceded that slavery was *the* cause of the Civil War, with a heavy emphasis on the moral dimensions of slavery, the tremendous suffering, inequality, and ongoing damage it caused, and even a debate today about possible reparations. However, recent statistical research by Paul

Collier and Anke Hoeffler has discovered that certain economic and demographic factors are related to the occurrence of modern civil wars such as income, population, ethnic division, natural resources, and exports. Statistically speaking, low income and high population increased the probability of civil war, but, more important, countries that had a high share of primary exports compared to GDP (gross domestic product, or national income) were more likely to experience a rebellion. Natural resources, such as mines and productive farmland, increased the risk of war: "We interpret this as being due to the taxable base of the economy constituting an attraction for rebels wishing to capture the state," but it could also encourage secession. These comprehensive results fit the American Civil War. The South had a large natural resource base in its farmland, which produced primary exports such as cotton and tobacco. Interestingly, this research also found that in their analysis of the causes of civil wars, "greed" was a better explanation than "grievance" between racial and tribal groups.[1] Thus, the American Civil War is not separate and unique from the pattern of human history related to civil wars, and this argument supports the case for economic theory's role in improving our understanding of this central event in American history.

Many readers of this book will have completed at least an introductory course in economics. For both those who did and those who did not, we provide a sketch of the basic concepts or ideas that illuminate the causes, conduct, and consequences of the Civil War. Some may be familiar and others less so.

OPPORTUNITY COST, SPECIALIZATION, AND TRADE

Economies have benefited from specialization and trade for at least the past 10,000 years. Indeed, both historical and modern economies depend critically on the proper evaluation of the opportunity cost of using resources in making economic production decisions or even in taking ordinary actions. Historical evidence clearly supports the notion that societies that "exploit" their human and natural resources eventually fail, while societies where individual property owners can efficiently calculate the use of their resources thrive and succeed. Resources may be devoted to making guns or Mercedes automobiles or to building new and better roads or to improving DVD technology. Individuals may spend more time gardening or reading, working or playing, but, in general, there is a limit to how much more of anything we can do. That limit is a constraint on our behavior. Thus, we as individuals must make adjustments at the margin: more tennis or more studying but not both in unlimited quantities. To do one task is to engage in a cost—the pleasure we might have had doing something else. Our particular choices culminate in the whole economy making "choices" at the margin: more guns means less butter.

Economists have a particular name for the situation facing individuals or economies described above. _Opportunity cost_ is the highest-valued alternative forgone in making any choice. The opportunity cost of a decision is the next most preferred or next-best alternative to a good or an activity (new clothes, going to chemistry class) that we must forgo in order to obtain some other good (a short vacation or extra sleep). During the Civil War, for example, the North and the South faced choices, individually and collectively. More iron for rails and nails meant less iron for ships and armaments. More fabric for uniforms meant less material for party dresses. For the individual, a decision to "join up" had a cost in terms of keeping the farm going. Whether it is hunting buffalo, harvesting trees, or sending soldiers into battle, resources will be exploited if decisions are based on distorted opportunity costs that are too low.

One of the reasons for the enduring interest in Adam Smith—the "father" of economics who wrote _The Wealth of Nations_ in 1776—is that he understood that the specialization and the division of labor created benefits for individuals and societies. _Division of labor_ refers to a situation in which the tasks associated with the production of a good or service are divided—and sometimes subdivided—and different individuals are assigned tasks that collectively bring about production of a good or service. As the division of labor takes place, societies and individuals develop _specialization_ where they become more productive in certain tasks and in particular goods based on abilities, training, and experience. Smith knew, for example, that we are far from being alike in talents or motivation. Just as there has always been specialization within the family unit owing to biology, among other factors, individuals' propensities lead to specialized careers. Smith (and Plato long before him) asked the critical question of whether it is more productive for each individual or family to provide for their own needs or whether they should specialize and trade. The answer, both for individuals and societies, was clearly the latter. Through trade and exchange, it can be shown that all parties to trade are better off than before specialization and trade.

Virtually all nations specialize in the production of goods and services to varying degrees. Different endowments of resources, different technologies, and different talents of the people are all reasons for specialization. A key and critical point about this specialization is not to be missed, however. Specialization permits the "acquisition" of more and better natural resources and improved technology. The gains from specializing in and exchanging goods and services are, in effect, equivalent to acquiring or developing additional natural resources or capital. As Smith knew, and as all nations discover after specialization and trade, the division of labor leads to increased consumption opportunities without the use of any additional resources. Examples from modern life are instructive. In the United States there is no domestic production of certain commodities such as crude rubber and diamonds; the entire supply is imported. Exotic spices are not commercially grown in Canada, although they could be cultivated in greenhouses with huge expenditures on lighting, heating, and labor. Canada does, however, produce a fair proportion of the world's wheat. Likewise, no wheat is grown on the tiny Caribbean island of Grenada, but nutmeg and other spices are. The point is that a number of factors, such as climate and resource base, provides a source of specialization and trade and that such trade is like an infusion of resources to countries who do not try to produce everything themselves. To be successful, specialization must be based on opportunity costs, for if Canada specialized in nutmeg it would surely perish.

This simple principle leads to the advocacy, at least among most economists, of complete free and unencumbered trade between countries and regions. One of the fiscal principles of the new nation of the United States was a reliance on tariff revenues to support the expenditures of the federal government but completely free trade among the individual states. This revenue-getting device may have had benefits in terms of providing income, but it also limited the gains that the fledgling country could obtain from trading with other countries. Generally, moreover, it can be shown that the losses to consumers from tariffs outweigh the gains in tax revenues to government combined with the protection from competition that it provides domestic industries. Tariffs during the antebellum period reduced the amount of profitable specialization and trade and were a major source of sectional political conflict. The South generally supported low tariffs and, for several reasons, Northern interests supported high tariffs. While greatly diminished in modern times due to the immense size of the American economy, tariffs are still a major source of conflict in domestic and international politics.

SUPPLY AND DEMAND

What motivates you or any other individual to buy or sell some good or service or to do anything, for that matter? Immediately, one thinks of the price. Perhaps the oldest and most durable inquiry in economics is the attempt to more fully answer this question. The simple answer, as one can teach a parrot, is supply and demand. If supply and demand explain market values, what, then, is a market? A market is any collection of buyers and sellers exchanging goods and services, labor, and resources where a price is generated by continuous buyer-seller interaction. Markets may be highly organized, such as the New York Stock Exchange or the Chicago Commodities Exchange, or loosely organized, such as the buying and selling of used cars out of the newspaper. Prices may be explicit, such as the posted prices of gasoline down the block from your house, or implicit, such as in religious services or in the marriage or dating "market." Whatever the market, it is supply and demand that determines the movement of prices up or down.

The question of motivation to buy or sell is the key to understanding this oldest of economic tools. Surely, you, as a demander or supplier, are motivated by price. But it is also true that the collective actions of demanders and suppliers determine where price will be (what price you will have to pay for something). This seeming paradox is resolved by understanding a few underlying principles. A demand curve for an individual is a hypothetical schedule or list of what you would *want* to buy given such a list, with all other factors remaining the same (economists call this condition *ceteris paribus*, meaning with all other things the same). Similarly, a supply curve for an individual supplier is based on a hypothetical schedule of what he would desire to sell given a list of possible selling prices, again with all other factors remaining the same. At high prices a consumer is willing to buy less than at low prices. At low prices a supplier is willing to offer fewer goods, services, or resources than at higher prices. When all buyers' demands and sellers' supplies are taken into account, a market price can be determined by the relative strength of the desires of buyers and sellers.

Clearly, then, it is price that is the proximate motivator of buyers and sellers in markets. But what underlies these "desires" to buy or sell at particular prices? That is, what underlies the demand and supply plans or the desire to buy and sell stuff? For demanders, a number of factors are important, particularly income. A change in income will obviously affect purchases. For some goods, a rise in income will increase the demand for beefsteak; for others, such as squash or turnips, it may even decrease demand. Those who have studied economics will recognize this difference between beefsteak and turnips as a contrast between the category of *normal* goods and the category of *inferior* goods. Normal goods are those products and services for which demand increases (decreases) with increases (decreases) in income. In contrast, the demand for inferior goods actually decreases (increases) with increases (decreases) in consumers' income. During the War Between the States, there was a general decline in income in both the North and the South, with certain groups such as gunmakers and blockade-runners gaining significantly while the general population on both sides suffered. The impact of price and income changes on the consumption of luxuries and inferior substitutes is a significant part of the economic story of everyday life during the Civil War.

Then there is the matter of how well other goods or services complement or substitute for a particular item. The relation depends on how goods are generally used by consumers. Take coffeemakers. If the demand for coffee pots, as would be supposed, is closely related to coffee beans, a doubling of the price of coffee beans would have an effect on the demand for coffee pots. In fact, it would depress or decrease the demand (the whole demand curve) for coffee pots with a price-lowering effect. This correlation would mean that coffee and coffee makers are *complements* in consumption. Complements are products that are related so that an increase in the price of one will decrease the demand for the other, or a decrease in the price of one will increase the demand for the other.

What if consumers consider coffee and tea substitutes? In the South during the Civil War the availability of coffee was severely curtailed with a dramatic rise in price. Tea was considered a substitute, as were certain types of tree bark, chicory, and persimmon seeds. The demand for these substitutes increased, and their prices rose. Substitutes, then, are products that are related so that an increase in the price of one will increase the demand for the other, or a decrease in the price of one will decrease the demand for the other. Our book will include many such situations from the history of the Civil War. As in all wartime periods, shortages (and sometimes surpluses) build up—situations that affect not only the price of the particular commodity but also the prices and quantities available of other related commodities. As we will see, for example, England was importing vast quantities of raw cotton from the South before 1861. When the South levied a de facto cotton embargo on England and the Union blockaded Southern ports, England turned to substitutes such as cotton from Egypt, among other places, as well as wool and hemp and other fibers. However, the prices of these substitutes rose significantly, resulting in rising product prices and unemployment for English textile manufacturers.

Other factors cause increases or decreases in consumer demand as well. If we expect prices to be lower in the future, for example, our demand for the item will tend to decrease in the present. Such *expectations* of all kinds affect demand. Higher anticipated incomes also affect the demand curve. If we expect incomes to be higher next month, next year, or next decade, we may consume more in the present (our demands shift rightward). A poor medical student may buy a Porsche, borrowing most of the money to do so, in anticipation of high incomes once she is in practice. In contrast, if we anticipate losing our job in the future, we will tend to curtail consumption in the present. Changes in the quality of goods or services may also affect demand for them. Changing the amount of ice or sugar in a twelve-ounce soft drink, for example, will alter the quality of the drink, and this difference in quality will alter the demand curve. In short, changes in income, price of related goods, expectations, or quality (plus other factors we have not considered) create shifts or changes in demand curves. And these changes will have predictable effects upon price.

Supply will, like demand, change (increase or decrease) when a number of nonprice factors change. The most important influence on the position of the supply curve is the cost of producing a good or service. The price of resources—labor, land, capital, managerial skills—may change as may technology or production or marketing techniques peculiar to the product. Any improvement in technology or any reduction in input prices would increase supply; that is, it would shift the supply curve to the right. As with demand, where consumer expectations about prices and income affect demand, the supply curve may be affected by sellers' expectations.

What are the effects of these behavioral shifts? If other factors such as consumers' income, the prices they face for substitutes or complements, or expectations do not remain the same, the demand for products or services increases or decreases. If supply remains stationary, anything that increases demand also increases the market price and quantity exchanged of the item, and anything that decreases it reduces the price and quantity. Similarly, if supplier or producer behavior changes because other factors do not remain equal, price and quantity changes will occur. A lowering of the cost of production for any reason will increase supply, decreasing the price and increasing the quantity of the good or service exchanged. A rise will have the opposite effect. Taxes, regulations, and greater risk to capital and profits all have the effect of reducing the supply of a good.

Demand and supply are powerful tools that help us to understand what has happened and what will happen in markets, that is, how prices and quantities will behave whether we are looking at the price of gasoline today or the price of coffee and cotton during the Civil War. To summarize, all nonprice factors that increase demand have price-raising and quantity-increasing effects in markets; all factors that decrease demand have price-lowering and quantity-decreasing effects. All nonprice factors affecting supply will have a final impact on price and quantity in the following form: factors such as lower costs of production or technological improvements will increase supply, lowering price and increasing quantity; all factors that decrease supply will raise price and lower quantity.

One last and important point should be made about demand and supply and the motivations of consumers and suppliers. Both demanders and suppliers react on the basis of relative prices, that is, the price of one good relative to other goods. In this book we consider a special and somewhat counterintuitive case of relative prices when goods are close substitutes in consumption but of different quality. Some economists refer to this as the case of shipping the good apples out. The principle is simple: if two qualities of apples are produced in Washington State and if transportation costs are the same for both, what kind of apple will be demanded in other parts of the country? You might be tempted to think that Floridians might choose the lower-quality apples from Washington if forced to pay the high transportation fees of shipping those apples across the country. However, if one adds a fixed cost such as freight charges to the price of apples at the point of origin (Washington), the *relative price* of the better apples is reduced relative to the poorer-quality ones. Thus a large proportion of the higher-quality apples will be exported. This same reasoning probably explains why many restaurants in Texas, a major cattle-producing state, specialize not in the choice and tender cuts of beef but in barbeque made with the brisket, generally considered one of the least desirable cuts. This principle, as we shall see, may be carried over to the fixed cost created by the risks of running the Union blockade. Relative prices therefore explain how the blockade encouraged runners to import luxury goods into a progressively poorer country, a result we have dubbed the Rhett Butler Effect, after the fictional blockade-runner in *Gone With the Wind*.

xxiv   INTRODUCTION

THE QUANTITY THEORY OF MONEY

People throughout history have been fooled into thinking that higher prices are the result of speculators who corner the market and drive up prices in all markets. Inflation of prices, however, is the result of too much money chasing too few goods. Economists study the relationship between money and prices beginning with the Quantity Theory of Money. With a set amount of goods, an increase in the quantity of money will lead to higher prices. During the Civil War both Union and Confederate governments switched from gold to paper and greatly expanded the quantity of money. Given that the quantity of goods decreased, prices increased dramatically, which greatly disturbed the organization and flow of economic activity in both the North and South.

RENT SEEKING AND INTEREST GROUPS

The term "interests" appears often in this book. What do "interests" have to do with economics and the Civil War? Antislavery or abolition groups were an interest, as were combinations of business or labor to obtain protective tariffs from the government; groups of investors or speculators in railroads seeking regulation were an interest, as were slaveholders. These groups were all interested in affecting income distribution through the political process. In economics, the political activity of interest groups is called *rent seeking*, which is the socially costly pursuit of wealth transfers. The traditional welfare loss associated with tolls, tariffs, and excise taxes, in addition to monopoly in the private sector, is due to the fact that these devices create prices in the economy that are above the marginal cost of producing goods and services. Rent-seeking losses are reductions in social welfare associated with the attempts by interest groups to secure monopolization of markets by competing for rents, or profits that can be created by the political process.[2]

Rent-seeking losses generally take place through a political process, but the concept has been extended to any activity where competition takes place for a fixed prize. The losses may include spending on lawyers and on lobbying or any other expenditure necessary to obtain the fixed "prize." Suppose, for example, that today a group of northern U.S. textile (or coal) manufacturers organize in order to lobby Congress in Washington for regulations, special tax privileges, or protective import tariffs. There would be clear costs to this activity, but what is the nature of the economic waste? Legal and lobbying resources are deflected from positive-sum employment to, at best, zero-sum activities. The waste is the opportunity cost (see above) of the resources devoted to lobbying in terms of the goods and services that they could have produced if used in other parts of the economy. Naturally, there will be "defensive" expenditures—actually, defensive costs—on the part of those whose welfare is being reduced. When added together these costs can be small or large to the overall economy. Individuals and groups whose rents are being threatened want to minimize costs. Those who stand to benefit, such as lobbyists and lawyers, want rent-seeking costs to be large. The actual results depend on how much control (legislative, executive, and judicial) is given to government over property rights by the constitution and constituents of any state.

Organization of any interest is costly and is the key to understanding how particular regulations or rules over property either are or are not enacted. The use of real resources to obtain a rent transfer from one group of (generally less organized) market participants to another group (often well organized and smaller in number) with intense interest in obtaining the monopoly prize creates social wastes and limits exchange. The wastes of rent seeking—wealth dissipation—are in contrast to the pursuit of profits and wealth production with no devices to redistribute wealth. An unregulated monopolist directs resources to the most valued ends and, in the process, makes profits. He or she creates wealth. A competitive process, so long as entry is not barred, ensures that new and competing products reduce profit margins over time. Society's welfare is thereby maximized in contrast to the dissipation of resources and wealth experienced via rent seeking.

This theory of the rent-seeking process through interest group activity has no more important application than to history and historical institutions. Two contributions are of primary relevance. Rather than simply assuming that regulation was in the public interest, George Stigler began to develop a theory of institutional change by arguing that political systems were rationally devised and rationally employed to capture the regulatory apparatus. Industries demand regulation, in Stigler's theory, and the state supplies it through subsidies, entry control, suppression of substitutes and complements, price fixing, and other means. The political process through which politicians are able to "sell" regulations for votes and resources makes it unlikely that the public interest will prevail. Characteristics of the voting process—most particularly the fact that the voter needs an agent and cannot vote for herself on marginal issues—lead to all kinds of agency problems. Only strongly felt preferences of majorities and minorities are registered. Some voters, even a large number, remain rationally ignorant since the pro-rata effect on them of particular forms of regulation is perceived to be small or nonexistent.[3] Textile consumers in the pre-Civil War era were, in effect, taxed by tariffs, but only on a relatively small pro-rata basis and thus were unable to form defensive interest groups to combat the strongly organized industrial groups that lobbied the antebellum Congress.

Sam Peltzman, in a generalization of Stigler's theory, developed a model including the marginal tradeoffs by politician-regulators in an interest group setting that accounted for both producers' and consumers' surplus distributions.[4] Net demanders of regulation, represented by interest groups *of any kind*, were wedded to politician-suppliers of regulation in a general theory integrating economic factors with the political process. Here, rent seeking is the essence of the process through which regulations appear (and disappear). Those who seek regulation are typically members of an industry or profession seeking self-regulation that provide the interest groups with barriers to entry and protection from competition. Successful groups tend to be relatively small and have well-defined common interests in order to organize effectively to obtain large benefits. Those injured by economic regulation are typically consumers who suffer small losses per person, who are large in number, and who lack well-known and well-defined interests. The important and often neglected point is that the resources devoted to rent seeking—lobbying, legal expenses, and so on—are wasted resources from the standpoint of society. In this non-Marxian process, consumers or any other group can "win." The trick of the politician-regulator (monarch or dictator) is to balance the regulatory favors of one group against the other, but, in doing so, property rights, incentives, and the volume of exchange are altered, reducing wealth creation. This process, with particular situations clearly described, becomes a theory of government or institutional-historical change. Rents and potential rents emerge through technological change that can support new regulations, deregulation, or a cycle of interventions. Once some political metric and constitutional conditions are assumed, such as monarchy or democracy, the theory of rent seeking along with particular forms of self-interested behavior are capable of explaining many important aspects of historical processes.

Competition for fixed "prizes" must have occurred from the very dawn of humankind. There are undoubtedly numerous and important examples of rent-seeking activity in primitive and early societies. Monarchy, authoritarian rule, and dictatorships—systems that punctuated ancient, medieval, and early modern worlds—were cultures ripe for rent seeking. So were the antebellum and Civil War societies in the United States. Rent-seeking interest groups emerged during the beginnings of U.S. constitutional government and even earlier in America. Groups organized and lobbied the federal and state legislatures on all manner of rules, regulations, and privileges. The advent of the railroad brought railway subsidies in the form of land and bond guarantees. The admission of states to the Union was cause for intensive lobbying for or against the legality of slavery. Tariff issues were always a source of conflict between North and South. During the Civil War the Confederate and Union governments were the nexus through which often intense lobbying took place. Attempts to stem blockade-running of "luxury goods" (including whiskey) were the source of a series of rent-seeking legislation. Particularized interests often dominated the general welfare before, during, and after the Civil War. In sum, the rent-seeking/interest group theory is a useful tool to employ in analyzing the economics of the Civil War.

WHAT YOU MIGHT GAIN BY READING THIS BOOK

We hope that you enjoy reading this book, but the strength of economic analysis is explanatory value, not entertainment. After reading it, you will have both an understanding of how economic issues were a driving force in the events of the Civil War and an appreciation of how economic theory is useful in understanding historical events. Here are some of the specific items of knowledge found in the book:

- The Civil War is often painted as irrational, illogical, or inevitable. Economics shows us that man is rational and logical but must make decisions in unique political and economic environments under specific constraints and with imperfect knowledge. History, therefore, can often be usefully understood as a series of cause-and-effect events.
- Knowledge of economic issues is helpful in understanding the factors that led to the Civil War.
- Ideology is vital to understanding history, but it is also important to know the economic interests behind those ideologies.
- Grand battles, glory, heroism, and military tactics make for great and inspiring stories, but the keys to modern war are more basic issues such as the allocation of capital and labor, international trade, the functioning of markets, and the ability of an economy to provide logistical support.
- The war at sea was the decisive factor in both a military and economic sense. The land war was a stalemate, but the blockade was a decisive victory, and when it was completed, the Confederate army disintegrated and the Confederate government collapsed.
- (◉) The Confederate government was itself responsible for making the Union blockade effective.
- Many Confederate leaders had a states' rights and limited-government ideology but fought the war with a powerful central government. Union leaders, in large measure, advocated a big-government platform but fought the war by turning more to the market and relative fiscal prudence.
- (◉) Northerners and Southerners both blamed businessmen, blockade-runners, and speculators for rising prices, but the real cause was government. Paper money inflation, trade restrictions, war-related output reductions, and the uncertainties of war caused higher prices. Incidentally,

the evidence presented here helps decide a long-standing debate in monetary theory.

(•) War is always and everywhere bad for the economy. The Civil War interrupted one of the greatest economic expansions in world history and continued to have a depressing effect on the economy until at least the next great crisis period in American history, the Progressive Era and World War I.

• Do you know who coined the term "Yankee ingenuity," when the New Deal began, who the real-life Wizard of Oz was, how the South got its famous nickname of Dixie, or what the real-life Rhett Butler did give a damn about? Answers to all five questions are important components of the economics of the Civil War.

In addition, this book can improve your understanding of nineteenth-century America and beyond because it integrates an analysis of the great ideological forces with an analysis of the major institutional changes of the century.

NOTES

1. Paul Collier and Anke Hoeffler, "On Economic Causes of Civil War," *Oxford Economic Papers* 50 (1998): 571; Paul Collier and Anke Hoeffler, "Greed and Grievance in Civil War," Working Paper, 2000.

2. Robert B. Ekelund Jr. and Robert D. Tollison, "The Interest-Group Theory of Government," in *The Elgar Companion to Public Choice*, ed. William F. Shughart II and Laura Razzolini (Cheltenham, UK: Edward Elgar, 2001), 357–78; Robert D. Tollison, "Rent Seeking: A Survey," *Kyklos* 35 (1982): 575–602.

3. George J. Stigler, "The Theory of Economic Regulation," *Bell Journal of Economics and Management Science* 2 (Spring 1971): 3–21.

4. Sam Peltzman, "Toward a More General Theory of Regulation," *Journal of Law and Economics* 19 (August 1976): 211–40.

CHAPTER ONE

ECONOMIC INTERESTS AND THE ONSET OF THE CIVIL WAR

The Tariff

In the years between 1832 and 1860 there was great vacillation in the tariff policy of the United States; there were also great fluctuations in the course of trade and industry.
—Frank W. Taussig, *The Tariff History of the United States* (1888)

WHY THE CIVIL WAR?

"WAR IS HELL," as Yankee general William Tecumseh Sherman put it. And after war is done—in the horrible wake of death and devastation—it is important to "spin" or cloud the reason or reasons for it. Therefore, it is often difficult to determine with great precision the original reason or reasons for war.

The Civil War was such a conflict. While the victors usually write the history of events, it is nonetheless clear that the mass of contemporary writings on the Civil War emphasizes different and sometimes contradictory positions on "causes." The moral outrage of slavery and the whole slave system introduced into the American colonies long before the midnineteenth century receives the lion's share of attention now. Romantic and dramatic critiques of slavery—embodied perhaps in literary works such as *Uncle Tom's Cabin* in 1851 and in early slave revolts such as Nat Turner's Rebellion in the early 1830s—are weighed in a good deal of contemporary work. For their part, some economists have also concentrated on the impact of the slave economy on the efficiency and profitability of the system, the most famous being the analysis of Robert Fogel and Stanley Engerman in *Time on the Cross* (1974).

1

Black slavery was a central moral and political reason for war, with a majority of Northerners opposing it and a majority of Southerners supporting it. Indeed, slavery and its opposition were interwoven into the economic, political, social, and religious fabric of America. However, it was not the only factor in the South's decision to secede and the North's decision to take up arms to prevent secession. Active abolitionists in the North and slaveholders in the South were relatively small minorities of their populations. Therefore, to get below the surface of these issues we focus on economic interests in the various causes that have been attributed to the Civil War. The evolving relations between the powers of the federal government and the states were certainly an issue. In general, the South's well-known position was one of states' rights, while the North increasingly preferred a stronger central government. This question was the underpinning of another incendiary matter—the issue of import duties. Both as a revenue device for the federal government and as a means of industry protection, the tariff was a flashpoint for particular interests, North and South.

The view that the Civil War and other grand events in American history were essentially economic contests is often referred to as the Beard Thesis after the influential American historian Charles Beard and his wife, Mary. Here, economic interests and forces are an essential determining factor in history, a view shared by such disparate groups as the Marxists and the Public Choice School in economics. While support for this perspective has changed over time, new evidence concerning economic interests and party affiliation in the North in the years leading up to the conflict has established new support for the Beard Thesis as applied to the Civil War.[1]

We maintain that a multiplicity of issues brought about the conflict and that those economic interests and the interest groups surrounding them were the key factor in explaining these events. While we acknowledge that other dimensions affected the coming of the war, such as the moral and philosophical horrors of slavery, this chapter argues that economic interests, many of them at least somewhat related to slavery, were a major factor in the emergence of the conflict. Political parties, moreover, evolved and coalesced around this embroidery of interests. Many social and economic factors are involved in this connection, including the status of money and banking in the North and South, canal and railway building, and other public works. These issues will all be discussed as our book proceeds. In the present chapter, however, we focus on the interest group economics of a major issue: the tariff. We rely on a wealth of materials on the Civil War by economists. As you will see, interest groups expressed through political parties reached an impasse in the late 1850s. Economic interests, contrary to more naïve analyses, were not geographically "sectional" in nature but were based on common economic interests both North and South.

POLITICS IN THE NEW NATION, 1820–1860

In early America, politics were more fluid and far less regularized than they are today. The inherited English-like parties (Whigs and Federalists) were in a process of evolution during the early years of the Republic and became far more complex as interest groups developed the political landscape. Dominant leaders of the period included such men as Andrew Jackson, who opposed the federal banking system and "declared war" on the Second Bank of the United States, and Henry Clay, who was the major proponent of the "American system" of public works, protectionism, and a government bank. The career of South Carolina's John C. Calhoun is a good example of the rapid pace of change in the new nation. Calhoun supported a strong national government early in his career but later became the leader in defense of free trade, states' rights, and slavery. The views of these men, together with the economic interests they represented, shaped the ever-changing face of politics.

Federalists such as Alexander Hamilton and John Adams, supporters of a strong central government, were the predecessors of the Whigs, who were generally proponents of high tariffs and big government in Washington, DC. The Democrats—called Democratic-Republicans under Thomas Jefferson—were the successors to the anti-Federalists, such as John Taylor of Caroline, who extolled a decentralized system of limited government based, at least initially, on an agrarian conception of production. Taylor even coined the term "capitalist," not to refer to an entrepreneur but rather to someone who capitalized on government-granted privileges, monopolies, and protectionism at the expense of ordinary citizens.[2] As interests changed, splinter groups from the two major parties would merge to form other parties. Issues such as tariff protection, the expansion of slavery into new territories, and the question of whether the federal government should give land away free of charge engendered all kinds of political activity prior to 1860. The Republican Party that emerged in the 1850s was an amalgamation of historical influences, third parties, and interest groups.

The concept of the federal provision of land, rather than its sale, captured the interest of a group opposed to the extension of slavery called the Free-Soil Party. By the late 1840s the Free-Soil Party had attracted the abolitionist and slavery "containment" Democrats. As is common in today's third parties, Free-Soil candidates had modest political successes of their own but were able to influence elections, notably that of the last Whig presidency (1849–1853). Zachary Taylor died in office in 1850 and was succeeded by Millard Fillmore.

In addition to the Free-Soilers, another interest group was opposed to open immigration and immigrant labor. The period 1820–1860 was one of intense immigration with close to six million people added to the U.S. population, largely from Catholic Ireland and from Germany. One-half of New York's population was composed of immigrants at this time, and the city would experience a major, bloody riot by mostly Irish laborers in 1863 in protest against the military draft, which threatened to dissolve the Union. The ready availability of immigrant labor, the competition for jobs, and the fear of the immigrants' emerging political power created a party based largely on xenophobia (literally, a fear of foreigners). This Protestant crusade of nativists against Roman Catholics became known as the Order of the Star Spangled Banner and the Know Nothing Party. (Echoes of xenophobia may be heard today in anti-immigrant sentiment or in economic slogans such as "Buy American.") When questioned about their political affiliations, members were instructed to keep their deliberations secret and claim to "know nothing."

As with the Free-Soilers, the Know Nothings had less political success on their own than they had when finally agglomerated into a new party in 1854 called the Republicans. That party, which fielded candidate John C. Frémont in the 1856 election, was the product of these splinter parties plus Whigs, disaffected Northern Democrats, and Westerners. Generally speaking (and there are significant exceptions), their interests included support for free land for settlers, nonextension of slavery into new territories, protectionism for industry, a national bank, a large national debt, and a larger federal government engaged in extensive public works. However, we do not seek to paint a high contrast in regional politics. All Southerners were not Jeffersonians nor were all Northerners Hamiltonians. For example, Henry Clay was a slaveholding Southerner and Martin Van Buren was a Jeffersonian and a New Yorker. It is true that self-interest led a large number of people in the mid-Atlantic states to join the rent-seeking activities of the Whig Party. That party, however, was also strong among planters of the lower Mississippi Valley and even stronger in areas of Southern states such as North Carolina. The Whigs were viable and competitive in all of the pre-Civil War Southern states until the party system began to disintegrate due to stresses caused by slavery and secession.

The modern Democratic Party was established under Andrew Jackson, an immensely popular politician. It was an offshoot of Thomas Jefferson's Democratic-Republicans. As the Jeffersonian origins suggest, Democrats were of an agrarian orientation, attracting Southerners to the cause. States' rights versus the federal government as well as a small, central government in Washington financed with a low, revenue-generating tariff and federal land sales (land giveaways only intensified competition among farmers and increased demands for higher tariffs) were hallmarks of the party. Slavery and its expansion into emerging sections of the United States were also high on the agenda of most, but certainly not all, Democrats.

Again, complete bifurcation between the interests of Republicans and Democrats is not in order. It is true that by the 1850s, with the Second Party System of Democrats and Whigs already basically defunct, the Democratic administrations of Franklin Pierce and James Buchanan favored slavery and its expansion. But they were opposed by a major segment of the party led by Senator Stephen A. Douglas of Illinois, who was neutral on slavery.

Another major segment, antislavery Democrats, bolted and eventually helped to establish the Republican Party in 1854 in response to the Kansas-Nebraska Act. During the tumultuous political events, the economy was also undergoing radical change and rapid development.

GROWTH, TECHNOLOGY, AND LABOR

Economic growth in the highly agrarian but industrially developing economy is a matter of sharp debate. Whether there was a "take off" in the United States during the period 1820–1860—one corresponding to the earlier advent of the Industrial Revolution in England—is uncertain, and calculations depend heavily upon the time intervals covered. We do know that there were technological innovations and expansive economic development, and European observers, such as Alexis de Tocqueville, were very impressed with the progress of the new nation.

The consensus appears to be that the U.S. economy grew at an average long-run rate of about 1.3 to 1.5 percent per year with higher growth rates observed in the latter part of the period. Table 1-1, adapted from statistical research by Paul A. David, shows no startling changes in growth rates over the entire 1800–1860 period.[3] While real Gross National Product varied greatly over 20-year intervals, growth rates in average per capita annual income increased close to 1.3 percent in the intervals 1800–1835 and 1835–1855 and over the whole time span from 1800 to 1860. These growth rates are respectable by historical and international comparisons. The economic standard of living would double every generation, or in fifty-three years at a 1.3 percent growth rate and every forty-six years at a 1.5 percent growth rate.

The U.S. economy was quite prosperous between 1846 and 1856 but slowed down after the Panic of 1857, particularly in the North. A large number of reasons have been offered for its causes, but money and banking problems were at its core. The trigger for the Panic was due in part to the reallocation of capital that had to take place in the North as the tariff levels were reduced from highly protectionist ones down to a "revenue tariff" of around 20 percent, which tended to maximize tariff revenues over the long run.

Table 1-1. Rates of Growth of Real GNP and Real GNP per Capita, 1800–1860

Intervals	Real GNP per capita Long-Term Trend Growth Rate (percent)	Real GNP (percent)
1800–1860	1.27	4.32
1800–1835	1.22	4.28
1835–1855	1.30	4.40
1800–1820	0.24	3.29
1810–1830	1.54	4.53
1820–1840	1.96	4.96
1830–1850	1.37	4.39
1835–1855	1.31	4.39
1840–1860	1.59	4.73

Source: Adapted from Paul A. David, "New Light on a Statistical Dark Age: U.S. Real Product Growth before 1840," *American Economic Review* 57 (May 1967): Table 1, 297.

Growth in the early American economy was based on the attraction of low-cost fertile land in an institutional framework that defined and enforced an individual's property rights. This land attracted wage labor from Europe and slave labor from Africa. Immigration, beginning as a trickle of little more than 8,000 people in 1820, increased to 114,000 in 1845. From 1845 to 1855 well over three million people entered the country. Added to this flow of immigration was the domestic population growth. The black population continued to expand rapidly even after the importation of slaves was constitutionally banned after 1808. Also important was the willingness of people to move within the country for the best economic opportunities. The backbone of this economic growth, however, was the development of the nation's capital stock, which included the clearing of land for farming, the building of houses and barns, and the creation of transportation networks such as canals and railroads.

Technological developments such as the application of the steam engine to ships greatly expanded and enhanced transportation. The building of railroads began in the early 1830s, and there were more than 30,000 miles of track by 1860, a 15-fold increase over that in 1840. However, it is important to remember that not all railroad building had positive economic effects. Many of the roads were constructed during speculative credit booms or were based on government subsidy schemes, which often involved fraud and corruption, and as a result an abnormally high number of these railroads were unprofitable or bankrupt and therefore should be considered economic mistakes. History has clearly shown that the "build it and they will come" philosophy of economic development is a mistaken and very costly approach. Rational infrastructure investment such as railroads and ballparks are not the *cause* of economic development but a result. Nevertheless, the reduction in transportation costs, whether subsidized or not, had a large impact on the volume of exchange in the young American economy and helped integrate and expand the country. In short, new technologies such as the steam engine and the railroad were important factors in early American economic growth and development (much like the computer today), and their application took place in America at such a rapid pace because investors thought that these were the best places to risk their savings and capital and to expend their labor.

A number of anomalies exist concerning income and wage growth over the antebellum period, including claims of falling and stagnant wage growth. For example, economic historians have conjured up a statistical anomaly regarding a measured decline in the height and weight of Americans during the late antebellum time that would suggest it was a period of economic hardship. However, this and other anomalies are resolved by turning to the actual history of the period, which saw massive immigration, significant migration and urbanization, and a wave of religious fervor and prohibitionist policies that swept the nation.[4]

Using data from military hiring of civilian workers, Robert B. Margo found real wage growth during this period and that higher wages were tied to increases in productivity.[5] The economy was vibrant between 1846 and 1856 (a period that coincided with a great wave of immigration and lower tariff rates). Cyclical changes in labor demand and supply (especially immigration) along with changes in the technology of transportation, communications, and the factory system produced an era of relatively high growth and higher real wages. Further, long-run growth rates in white-collar wages were higher than those of common labor and artisans in all areas of the country.[6] This phenomenon was possibly a sign that immigration increased labor supply and restrained wage rates for common labor and artisans while the managerial class that directed the economy was in greater demand. Naturally, geography and the resource base played a role in income growth in the various regions of the nation. The urban and relatively industrialized Northeast contrasted with the agrarian South Atlantic region. On the eve of the Civil War, New Orleans was the only true Southern city in the top fifteen U.S. cities in population. As Douglass North describes the agrarian South,

> The nature of cotton production (and of tobacco, rice, and sugar production), and the economic and social consequences of investment in this form of capital, affected not only the economic structure of the area, but molded the pattern of settlement and urbanization and the distribution of income as well. The consequence . . . was that the expanding income from the marketing of these staples outside the region induced little growth within the South. Income received there had little local multiplier effect, but flowed directly to the North and the West for imports of services, manufactures, and foodstuffs.[7]

The nature of production and the locational patterns of trade—a triangular interregional trade between West, Northeast, and Southeast—were important in explaining income distribution and wealth flows between major regions of the country. While the North model has been questioned, interregional trade did permit each region to better develop its comparative advantages and thus generate greater incomes. While the West could produce foodstuffs for export to both regions, two critical economic issues affecting the North and South stand out in shaping the conflict: the tariff question and slavery.

ECONOMICS OF THE TARIFF

One of the critical domestic issues prior to the Civil War was the crazy quilt of the tariff structure of the United States between 1820 and 1860. Throughout English history, tariffs, or customs duties, collected on imports (and sometimes on exports) were regarded as a *regalian* right and royal prerogative, with revenues reserved to the monarch to carry out the necessary business of the realm. The same was true for a number of European nations.

Once an issue of contention leading to the American Revolution, taxation of imports was the chief source of revenue for the fledgling Republic. In the early days of the new nation, the country remained fundamentally agricultural in its basic economic organization. Tariffs were low at a general 5 percent on dutiable imports.

Civil War Timeline: The Tariff Question

1789–1808	U.S. economy basically agricultural as in colonial times. In 1789 a 5 percent import duty in force	
1808–1832	Tariff becomes the most important economic debate in the U.S.	
	1808–1815	Extreme protection with tariff (import substitution)
	1816–1824	A period of relatively free trade (but some duties still existed)
	1824	Protective tariff passes Congress
	1828	"Tariff of Abominations" (one of the most stringent protective tariffs in U.S. history)
	1832	Whig-Republican protective tariff enlarged
1832–1860	Tumultuous swings in tariff policies	
	1832–1833	South (state of South Carolina) attempts to nullify tariff of 1832
	1833–1842	In 1833 the Compromise Tariff Act is passed with gradual reduction of duties until 1842
	1842–1846	Protection of industries (cottons) under Whig-Republican dominance
	1846–1847	Democrats again lowered duties but "effected no more than a moderation in the application of protection," according to Taussig (1888: 318)
	1857–1860	Further reduction in duties in an approach to freer trade
1861	War begins	

Sources: Frank W. Taussig, "The Tariff, 1830–1860," *Quarterly Journal of Economics* 2 (April 1888); idem, *The Tariff History of the United States* (New York: G. P. Putnam's Sons, 1888).

Tariffs as a Revenue Device

As the nation grew, the tariff became the single most important domestic economic issue prior to the Civil War. It was a two-headed issue: the tariff was the primary source of revenue to the

Figure 1-1. Federal Expenditures by Category, 1820–1860

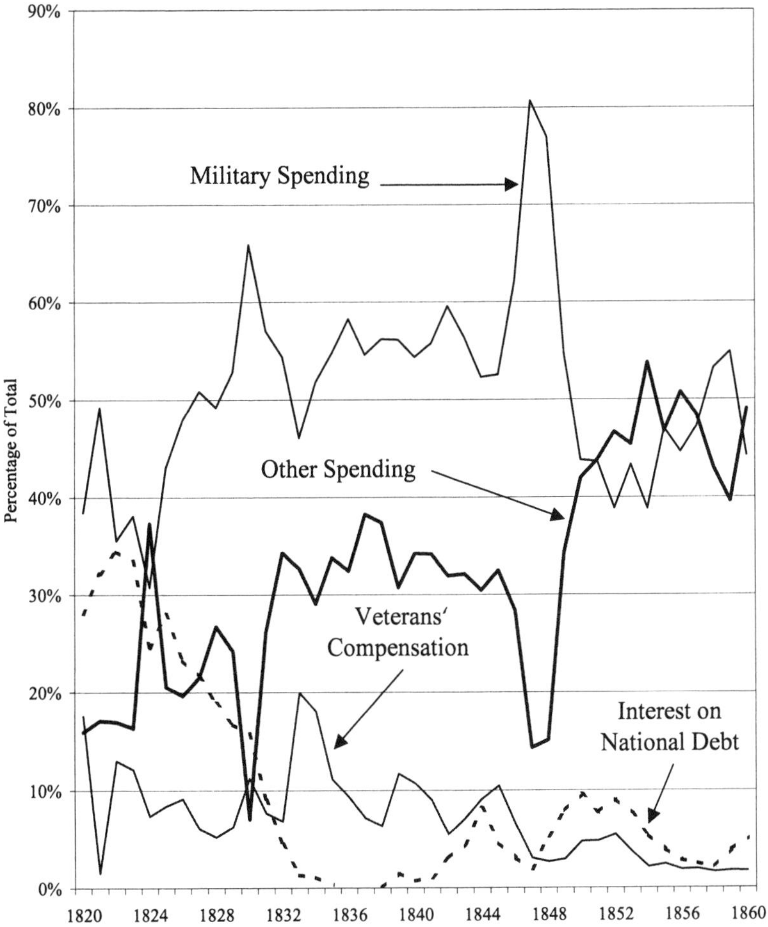

Source: U.S. Bureau of the Census, *Historical Statistics of the United States, Colonial Times to 1970* (Washington, DC: Bureau of the Census, 1975).

federal government, and it was a device to protect domestic industry. The importance of the tariff as a revenue device lay in the fact that it was the primary source of expenditure on all federally provided goods and services. A look at the sources of government revenue and government expenditures over the period 1820–1860 provides some idea of the directions of the federal accounts.

First consider expenditures, as shown in Figure 1-1. Clearly, direct and indirect military expenditures accounted for the mass of federal government outlays over the entire period. These expenditures, on the U.S. Army and Navy in addition to payments due to veterans of past wars, correspond historically to the primary role of government—the provision of the national defense. Since the philosophy of a balanced budget in the federal accounts was far more binding at the time, at least philosophically if not politically, interest payments on the public debt were relatively modest. Debt-financed spending was far less common than it is today. The "Other Spending," which was sometimes significant, included expenditures on roads, bridges, forts, and subsidies to other businesses dealing with infrastructure.

Customs duties derived from tariffs dominated government receipts as a source of income as shown in Figure 1-2, although the revenues from land sales (sales of public lands to private individuals) were a significant, if sometimes erratic, source over the 40-year period. Clearly, the dominance of customs duties as a source of the total revenue of the federal government was interrupted by land sales only twice over the period 1820–1860—once in the 1830s and again from 1853 to 1857. At all other times, the government relied almost completely on customs revenues derived from tariffs to finance federal expenditures.

Because there was no income tax and because reliance on internal revenues through other taxes was chiefly a wartime phenomenon, the issue of the tariff as a revenue source is highly important. As the following section reveals, tariffs were also the result of manufacturing and other interests seeking government protection from foreign competition as well as an increase in their revenues and income. As a revenue-producing device for government, Figure 1-2 suggests that the use of tariffs could be highly volatile and uncertain. A case in point concerns Americans' response to the Tariff of 1842, when higher rates resulted in lower revenues. This tariff was basically a device to protect American industry (see Civil War Timeline), but it was also hoped that the stiff increase in duties would help cover the deficits created in the federal accounts by the Panic of 1837. Instead, the elasticity of demand was such that the increase in price of cottons and other goods precipitated by the new tariff caused revenues from cus-

Figure 1-2. Federal Revenues by Category, 1820–1860

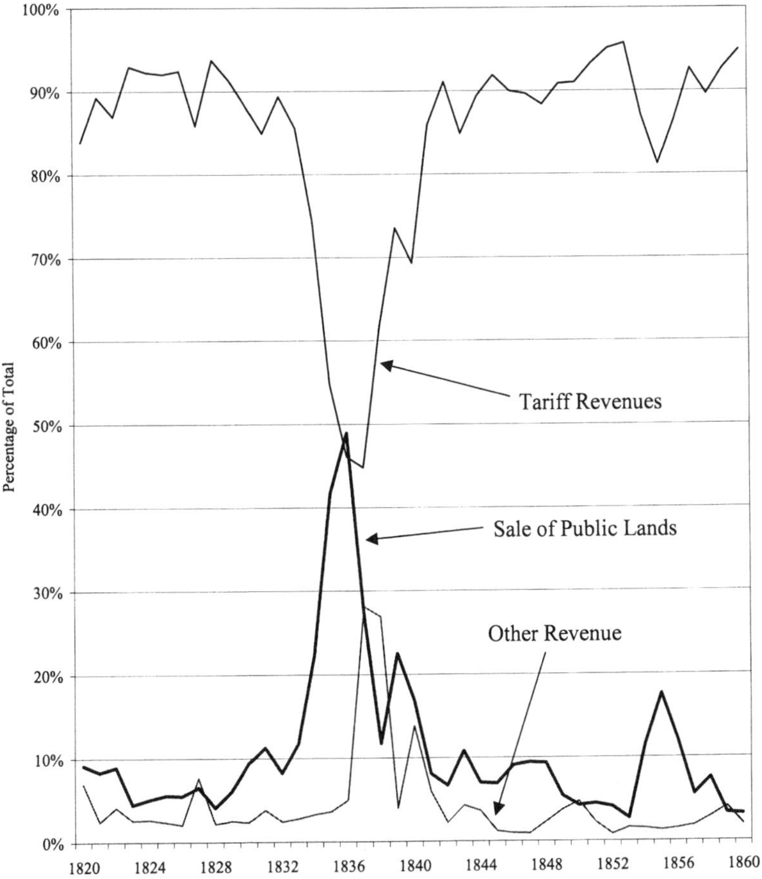

Source: U.S. Bureau of the Census, *Historical Statistics of the United States, Colonial Times to 1970* (Washington, DC: Bureau of the Census, 1975).

toms to fall drastically between 1842 and 1843 (see Figure 1-2). The secretary of the treasury in 1846 noted that this decline "rose from the prohibitory character of specific duties." Moreover, "the revenue under the tariff of 1842 must have continued to sink so rapidly as soon to have caused a great deficit, even though in time of peace, and thus have required ultimately a resort to direct taxes or excises."[8] The dramatic deficit caused by the Tariff of 1842 was in contrast to the huge rise in foreign trade (and customs revenues) created by the tariff reductions in 1846 and 1857.[9]

The problem in 1842 was that federal politicians were working under a reelection constraint, and that constraint virtually guaranteed that interest groups would affect the distribution of income through tariff protection.

Tariffs for Protection

Tariffs, of course, can do more than provide revenue for governments. When tariff rates do not follow the constitutional provision in Article 1, Section 8, that is, when rates are not uniform or the same on all goods, they often act as artificial barriers to trade. Free trade—despite the exceptions claimed in all ages and times, including pre-Civil War America—leads to maximum economic welfare among nations. Free trade and specialization expand consumption possibilities and deliver goods to consumers at the lowest possible costs. Despite the generalized benefits, some parties are harmed (in the short run) by free trade, and pressures are brought to bear on governments by producer groups for protection from foreign competition. Sometimes these groups win political favors, such as tariffs or quotas, to reduce the competitive threat. These favors, developed through the democratic political process, were known in the early days of the United States just as they are today. Restrictions on sugar imports, for example, benefit farmers but result in higher prices for consumers, both now and during the antebellum period.

Consider the process of protection in more detail. A tariff, by raising the imported price for an item above the (initial) domestic price, provides an umbrella from foreign competitors for domestic producers. Thus, domestic suppliers can raise their prices without any increase in costs. The higher price encourages domestic producers to increase output, which has the effect of raising domestic suppliers' profits (sometimes called "producer surplus"). The tariff also has the effect of raising employment *in that industry.* Consumers, on the other hand, suffer in the aggregate from the higher prices. Higher prices brought on by the tariff reduce benefits to consumers (sometimes called "consumer surplus") in the amount equal to the gain to producers, plus the increased government revenue, plus an additional deadweight cost that is lost to society in general. The deadweight loss results because there is a high opportunity cost for American sugar production relative to imported sugar, combined with the fact that some American consumers will switch to inferior substitutes, such as honey and maple sugar. In short, consumers lose more than the combined producers' gain and government revenue by the imposition of a tariff.

If tariffs reduce the general welfare of Americans, why (other than for revenue purposes) were they imposed in the early days of our Republic and why do we still observe them? The source of tariff protection is to be found in the urgings of merchants and manufacturers as well as from labor in domestic import-competing industries. Consumers, who lose a small pro rata amount from tariffs, are widely dispersed. It is costly for these groups to fight against tariffs and for free trade. To a consumer, for example, the tariff is a small part of the price of peanut butter. The incentive to organize and fight protective tariffs is therefore small.

The situation is different for producers. The pro rata share of the producer benefits from tariff protection are much higher among manufacturers because they are far fewer in number than consumers. Groups of producers, in their rational self-interest, lobby legislatures for special favors, such as tariffs on foreign imports. Thus, the interests of consumers and other groups in free trade are often sacrificed.

INTEREST GROUPS: NORTH AND SOUTH

Tariffs, for these and other reasons, were a political hot potato long before the modern age. Interest groups formed for economic reasons, some of them related to tariffs, from the very beginnings of America. Interest groups and opportunistic behavior riddled the American experience even in the colonial era. Rent-seeking interests in England, colonial governors in America, and favored merchants tried to impose all sorts of regulations on the colonists. For example, a Hat Act was passed in Parliament in 1732 under interest-group pressures from London felt makers. Already worried about French competition, these London businesses were fearful of the establishment of a hat industry in the northern colonies. The Act prohibited the exportation of hats from one colony to another, required colonists to serve a seven-year

apprenticeship before entering the trade, and barred the employment of Negroes in hatmaking altogether. But the ability of the
British government to deliver these rents to the London hatmakers
was illusory because the policies had to be enforced. Piracy, for-
mal and informal smuggling, and opportunistic behavior on the
part of the colonial government and bureaucratic apparatus kept
the British interest group from their reward. On the contrary, other
interest groups (North American hatmakers and some bureaucrats) appear to have won significant battles in this war of income
distribution.[10]

The South was basically an agrarian economy. This input-
producing region's major crops were tobacco, rice, and cotton,
with much of the latter intended for export or for the textile mills
of the North. Southerners had to earn their revenue to buy finished goods from the North and from abroad through the export
of raw materials. Since tariffs on finished goods, such as textiles
and luxuries, and on capital goods, such as machinery, raised the
prices paid by Southerners, they believed correctly that the "terms
of trade" were set against them by high protectionist tariffs. Thus,
from the earliest days of the nation, the tariff issue was paramount
to Southerners.

Naturally, some Northern interests had a different perspective. Some entrepreneurs supported high protective tariffs on the
basis of import substitution, using an "infant industry" argument
popularized by a number of American and European writers. Industries, in this view, need to be protected by high tariffs on imported products until the domestic industry "grows up."
Naturally, such tariffs did not benefit all Northerners; Northern
consumers were also harmed due to these tariffs. But among those
who prospered from protection were some Northern laborers as
well as the broader interests of the region, some of them urban,
from the spillover effects of the protective tariff.

The idea that protection in the form of tariffs, subsidies, and
quotas should be accorded to "infant industries" in developing
nations is an old one. The German politician-economist Friedrich
List (1789–1846) was one of the most important originators of the
argument in the nineteenth century. List, who came to America,
influencing writer-economist Henry Carey (1793–1879) on the
matter, argued that free trade that displaces either population or

domestic industry is undesirable. In effect, he and Carey (and Alexander Hamilton before them) maintained that economic resources must be safeguarded so that their future existence and development are assured. Modern variants of the idea of protection relate to the famous argument based on "economies of scale," which exist when, as plant size increases up to a point, long-run unit costs decline (which occurs when certain workers become more proficient at narrowly defined tasks) and machines are more closely tailored to individual processes. Careful econometric study shows that the role of "learning by doing" in the antebellum textile industry did not justify protection, which was almost exclusively in the interests of textile producers.[11] The "infant industry" argument is basically just a veil for protectionist interests and policies.

THE EXPENDITURE SIDE OF TARIFFS

Other groups had vested interests in increased government spending, not unlike today's interests associated with public education, national defense, or the space program. There were interests that wanted public works, such as federal guarantees for canal building or for the establishment of railroads. Most critical was the demand for expenditures on military-oriented goods, including "bricks for forts." Also there were interests encouraging transportation and interests favoring a federal infrastructure in Washington, DC. All of these groups had a bias in their political beliefs toward more federal spending, especially the Whigs, a big-government party that eventually became the Republicans. The Whigs, along with abolitionists and the Know Nothings (anti-black, anti-immigrant, pro-free land), formed the Republican Party in the 1850s.

In terms of government finance, another issue became of chief importance in the interest coalitions that led to the Civil War: the westward movement and the homesteading of lands in the expanding territories of what is now the Midwest. What began as a trickle at the beginning of the period became a land rush later in the century. As suggested in Figure 1-2, federal government revenues from land sales, while steady over the entire period 1820–1860, were a significant portion of federal revenues in 1835–36 and 1854–55. These sales were part of the battle of interests between North and South. Southerners tended to support land sales for two reasons, one direct and the other indirect: First, the revenues from land sales substituted for tariff revenues; and second, free land would increase the total supply of agricultural land, thus lowering land values in the South as well as the values of products produced on Southern acreage.

Generally speaking, therefore, the South supported balanced tariffs and land sales to finance a small federal government. On the other side, Northern interests supported high protective tariffs and federal land giveaways. Prior to 1860 these contrasting interests were represented in the political process by various movements and political parties that represented their interests in Congress. Democrats tended to support more of a balance between a revenue tariff and the selling of public lands to finance the federal government. The Whig Party and later the Republican Party advocated a high protective tariff to finance the federal government and "free land" for settlers. The Republicans also promoted high tariff rates as a means of redistributing income from the producers of exports, such as cotton, to the producers of goods protected by high tariffs, such as iron and manufactured items.

It is important once more to understand how this redistribution could take place. Since protective tariffs do more economic harm than good, the strength of members of the opposition would be expected to dominate. They would dominate if the costs of information and organization were zero or very low, but the costs are not low. Attempts to organize an interest group would be met with the so-called free rider problem—would an individual contribute to a lobbying effort against protective tariffs if she thought that others would do so? On the other hand, individuals who could profit from protection—producers and other groups—were much smaller in number and therefore had far lower organizational costs in terms of lobbying the federal legislature to obtain protection as well as a much larger benefit per producer.

Naturally, the particular social, political, and economic environment was a factor in the strength of these interests and in their ability to push legislation through Congress or to affect certain outcomes. Many industries, for example, claimed "infant industry" status. The "infants" demanded protection so that they could grow up to compete with goods imported from other countries. In terms of most early U.S. manufacturing, this claim was dubious. Another factor that always had some impact on many actual tariff enactments was "war status." Protecting the domestic economy in wartime or "protection for national defense" has been a perennial rationale for high tariffs throughout U.S. history, including the early years of the country. Thus, while there are always and everywhere interests in redistribution of wealth through political means, the events of the day weigh heavily on the ability of interests to obtain protection.

A BRIEF REVIEW OF THE ANTEBELLUM TARIFF

The antebellum tariff structure is important to an understanding of the timing and onset of the Civil War. Free trade, or the absence of tariffs and quotas, never existed in the United States. As the economy emerged from its agricultural nature, the benefits of using the tariff to gain redistribution became more apparent to producers of industrial goods, such as textiles and iron. Protection, along with federal revenue considerations, was always a part of the issue, but the years surrounding the War of 1812 brought on an enhanced taste for protection. As suggested in the Civil War Timeline, a period of relatively free trade ensued between 1816 and 1824, but in 1824 the first overtly protective tariff passed the federal legislature. As Frank Taussig argued and as verified in more recent research, the Tariff of 1824 and its companion passed in 1828 (the so-called Tariff of Abominations) were pivotal in solidifying economic interests in North and South. These economic interests and the uncertainty that attended them throughout the antebellum period, we argue, were a major factor in the coming of the Civil War in 1860.

In 1824, goods such as cotton textiles, paper, glass, woolens, and iron (including nails) were protected by taxes of 40 to 100 percent on the value of imports. This tariff, which was enacted when the U.S. Treasury was neither in surplus nor shortfall, aroused internal regional interests. Some idea of the kind of interests involved is given in the brilliant analysis of the 1824 tariff by Jonathan J. Pincus.[12] As Pincus reports, a bill similar to the

1824 Act missed passing the Senate by one vote in 1820, but in 1824 the high protective tariff passed 107 to 102 in the U.S. House of Representatives and 25 to 21 in the Senate.[13] While the raw vote is interesting, the breakdown of the vote by region tells the interest group tale.

The Tariff of 1824 sets out the interest groups and sectional interests through which tariff policy was established prior to the Civil War. Pincus's analysis of the votes for and against the tariff by states and regions is revealing.[14] The actual vote on the bill was the result of complex factors. The give and take on particular items—cottons, textiles, and iron—to be included was of great importance. A tariff benefiting one region was, generally speaking, a tax on another. Log rolling and vote trading took place as each representative and senator voted on the net effect on his constituents, on his own probability of election, and on maximizing his party's majority in the following congressional vote.[15]

While there was some concern that protective tariffs would be raised so high that customs revenues would be jeopardized and that higher internal taxes would have to be generated by a new set of domestic excise taxes, it was generally believed that customs revenues would support increased public works, including roads, canals, and, later, railroad building—a belief that had a large impact on the Western vote.

Table 1-2. House and Senate Votes on the Tariff of 1824

Region	House Vote		Senate Vote	
	Yea	Nay	Yea	Nay
New England	15	23	9	3
Mid-Atlantic	60	15	5	4
West	29	0	9	0
South	3	64	2	14
Total	**107**	**102**	**25**	**21**

Source: Jonathan J. Pincus, *Pressure Groups and Politics in Antebellum Tariffs* (New York: Columbia University Press, 1977), 62–63. © 1977 by Columbia University Press. Reprinted by permission of Jonathan J. Pincus.

Table 1-2 reveals that the vote on the 1824 protective tariff took place for the most part along sectional lines, with Senate "compromises" realigning votes to produce an overall 25-to-21 majority for the measure. Western interests were unanimously aligned in favor of the tariff, while the Southern states (with Tennessee's two votes the exception) were solidly against it. However, in New England the vote supporting the tariff was only 39 percent in the House but was 75 percent in the Senate. Both delegations from the mid-Atlantic states were in favor of the measure but by wildly differing margins. How may this be explained? Representatives vote on the particularized and often highly concentrated interests of their districts while senators take the broader voting interests of the entire state into account. As Pincus concludes, it is not small cohesive individual groups but larger diverse ones that are necessary in order to effectively lobby representatives and senators to obtain majority coalitions in such comprehensive legislation as the Tariff of 1824.

The use of the tariff for protection was the hallmark of the 1824 enactment, and it remained the central economic policy issue throughout the antebellum period. Northern manufacturers (their labor and other input providers) and Western laborers and settlers (on the revenue side of customs) favored protection while Southern planters and New England merchants (and shipping interests) opposed it. The Southern interests are succinctly described by Taussig and serve to underline the sources of the opposition to protective tariffs on Northern manufacturers right up to the Civil War. They came to understand that "manufactured goods must be bought in Europe or in the North, and that, wherever bought, a protective tariff would tend to make them dearer. Moreover, Cotton was not yet King, and the South was not sure that its staple was indispensable for the entire world. While the export of cotton on a large scale had begun, it was feared that England, in retaliation for high duties on English goods, might tax or exclude American cotton."[16]

Despite their opposition, the swelling of protectionist interests resulted in the passage of two of the highest protective tariff bills in U.S. history—the bills of 1828 ("Abominations") and 1832. A convention of protectionist interests was held in Harrisburg, Pennsylvania, in 1827 in support of higher tariffs, and by 1832 protectionism was in full bloom. The 1828 bill had revised tariffs using specific rates on particular items plus high *ad valorem* duties. The purpose was to heavily tax imported coarse wool (used to make carpets), cheap flannels, and cloth, all much used in the

South. The Tariff of 1832, passed by the Whigs or "National Republicans," greatly irritated Southerners (such as the one on coarse wool) because it imposed average rates on dutiable articles, including cottons and woolens, iron, and other goods, of 33 percent. Southerners launched a massive protest and nullification was advocated, particularly by the state of South Carolina. (Nullification was the refusal of a state to recognize or obey a law passed by the federal government.) Thus, the compromise Tariff Act of 1833 was enacted to mollify Southern interests (who, even at this date, at least voiced the possibility of secession).

That compromise promised the progressive lowering of tariffs through 1842, when there would be a uniform rate of 20 percent on dutiable imports. These lowerings, according to Taussig, were put into place very slowly and in willy-nilly fashion, and most of the reductions only took place in the first six months of 1842. Taussig's position was that tariffs had little effect on overall economic development in the antebellum United States, except in the crude iron industry, where, he argued, the tariff retarded the introduction of new methods of manufacture. He also made the interesting observation that rail iron was exempt from the tariff until 1842 due to the strength of a special-interest group concerned with the health and wealth of the nascent railway industry.

Although protectionist fervor had cooled, the Whigs supported and enacted a new protectionist bill in 1842, but the measure was reversed in the so-called Free Trade Act passed by the Democrats in 1846—an act that only moderated protection and partially mollified antiprotectionist interests in the South. However, by all accounts there was a period of prosperity between 1846 and 1857. Despite the Panic of 1857, which involved a banking and monetary crisis that might have threatened this prosperity, the tariff was again lowered due to surplus revenues in the federal treasury.

An important question then presents itself: With protection further moderated between 1857 and 1860, why was the tariff issue so critical a matter to Southern secession? A partial answer is "tariff uncertainty." Since tariffs took wide swings from high protection to more modern "free trade" levels over the period 1820–1860, manufacturers, merchants, and consumers were all uncertain of future prices and distributions of wealth. For their part, the agrarian Southerners were fearful of a politically driven return to high protective tariffs on manufactured goods. Northern and Midwestern manufacturing interests and investors were also uncertain concerning politically driven solutions and their profits. The complexity of the problem of "union" or "secession," moreover, grew with the reshuffling of political parties (Democrats and Republicans) over the 1850s and with the particularized interests that they represented.

Persuasive evidence that the Southern states took such "tariff uncertainty" seriously is revealed in a paper by Robert A. McGuire and T. Norman van Cott where the authors show that the Confederate constitution initiated a tariff clause that, at least in the wording, effectively prevented using import tariffs as a protective device and confined tariff rates to the "lower end of the Laffer curve."* Naturally, any import tariffs create some protection, but "the Confederate Constitution tells Confederate legislators to view promoting or fostering costs as the downside of raising tariff revenue. The resulting message is straightforward: tariffs above the revenue maximizing rate were unconstitutional." McGuire and Van Cott also note that the Morrill Act of 1861, which returned tariffs in the United States to 1846 levels and which was passed before the departure of Southern congressmen from the House of Representatives, was as much "a paramount objective of the Republican party and their protectionist allies at least since the Panic of 1857 and was a key plank in the August 1860 Republican party platform" as it was a revenue enhancer for the North.[17]

THE COMING OF WAR

Historians tell us that among the numerous causes that have been offered, the Civil War was basically fought over the issue of slavery, with the Union fighting to end black slavery and the Confederacy fighting to preserve it. Black civil rights leaders who advocate reparations for slavery argue that while Southerners

*The Laffer curve is a graph of the relationship between tax rates and tax revenues and shows that a low rate can generate the same revenue as a high protective tax rate.

were fighting to preserve the institution, the Yankees were for the most part fighting not to abolish slavery but for their economic interests and to preserve the Union. Whether or not it is judged the central moral issue, we argue that it had economic implications as well. Northern and Southern states were divided in terms of economic interests and politics, and this split generally coincided with the slave status of the states. Southern slaveowners were obviously interested in defending slavery because it allowed them to exploit income and wealth from the productivity of blacks to themselves. Evidence for slaveowners as an economic interest group is presented by Gerald Gunderson, who uses estimates of the value of slaves and the cost of the war to determine that the Southern states fought to defend slavery and the Northern states fought to abolish it. Gunderson clearly describes slavery as a central cause of the war. However, he argues that the South's secession need not have been a reaction against abolitionism but rather to "any program which implied some reduction in the returns from slave ownership," such as high tariffs, which would have threatened their self-interest.[18] As Gunderson notes,

> The reduction in the value of slaves within the Union, given Lincoln's election, measures the basic cause of the war. This is the "coercion" to which the southerners had frequently objected. It suggests that the Republicans were not viewed as abolitionists; that is, it was not expected that the slaves would be freed in the immediate future. It does represent a sizeable loss in slave values within the Union, however. Lincoln's election is foreseen as the beginning of an erosion in returns from bondsmen which is reflected in an immediate $700 million drop in their present value.[19]

Slaveholders can therefore be viewed as an economic interest group that established secession and thus helped precipitate the war. The very election of Abraham Lincoln was seen by them as an economic loss to slaveholders and as an impetus for secession and war. In other words, the containment policies of the Republican Party were a long-run threat to the wealth of slaveholders, but the party's protectionist policies were an immediate threat to the profitability of their plantations, having the same effect as one-third of the slave population running away outside the South.

The twin issues of tariffs and slavery were thus at the fore of aligning economic interest groups, North and South. The federal government enjoyed surpluses in the national accounts, and the tariff was lowered in 1857, despite strong opposition by iron manufacturers in Pennsylvania and wool producers in New England. Southerners remained fearful that Northern businessmen would turn the powers of the federal government against their wealth and interests to enrich Northern industries and monopolists. In all of the political battles among the various economic interests, slavery was the focal political, moral, and ideological issue, especially the debate over its extension into the expanding territories.

While these issues had been resolved politically for decades, the events of the 1850s foreshadowed the coming of war. In 1854, Democrat Franklin Pierce, supported the Kansas-Nebraska Act, which treated slavery as an exception to the Missouri Compromise of 1820, and earned the president and his party the enmity of Northerners because it was the North's position that slavery could be prohibited by Congress *before* a territory became a state. Southern Democrats, on the other hand, held that the decision should be made after statehood by a vote of the new state's citizens. With political parties destabilized, the new Republican Party organized and mounted a presidential candidate (Frémont) for the first time in 1856 against Democrat James Buchanan. The Republican Party was composed chiefly of anti-immigrant Know Nothings, anti-slavery Democrats (some of whom believed that slave power threatened or weakened the rights of free labor), and Northern manufacturing and industrial interests.

The economy was also tumultuous during the 1850s. Taken as a whole the decade was one of great economic growth and development. However, it was also a period of gold rushes, massive immigration, waves of speculation in land and railroads, and technological development. Then a banking "Panic" occurred in 1857. A failure of export demand for Western grains had put severe strains on banks. Then the Ohio Life Insurance Company failed to meet its bond obligations, and New York City banks suspended specie payments on October 13. The bank runs spread and caused banks all over the country to call in loans. Blame was placed on many quarters, including the new telegraph that spread

the dire information throughout the nation, and a sharp reces-
sion in economic activity ensued. While the exact impact of the
Panic on the emergence of the Civil War is in debate, there can be
no doubt that it helped precipitate an intensification of interests
already seething between North and South.[20]
    The emergence of the Republican Party—buttressed by calls
for tariff increases, slavery containment, and national control of
banks—was a clear threat to Southern interests. Slave power,
which threatened and cheapened (in some areas) wage labor, demanded states' rights against the federal government, and advocated land sales to finance the federal government fueled
Northern opposition. In an era of political and economic instability, the accumulated economic interests, now drawn along regional lines, precluded the possibility of compromise and set the
stage for war.

NOTES

    1. Mark Engel, "The Beards Were Right: Parties in the North, 1840–
1860," *Civil War History* 47 (2001): 30–56.
    2. John Taylor, *The Arator: Being a Series of Agricultural Essays, Prac-
tical and Political: In Sixty-Four Numbers*, edited and with an introduction by M. E. Bradford (Indianapolis: Liberty Classics, [1814] 1977).
    3. Paul A. David, "New Light on a Statistical Dark Age: U.S. Real
Product Growth before 1840," *American Economic Review* 57 (May 1967):
294–306.
    4. Mark Thornton, "Alcohol Consumption and the Standard of Living
in Antebellum America," *Atlantic Economic Journal* 23 (June 1995): 156.
    5. Robert A. Margo, *Wages and Labor Markets before the Civil War* (Chi-
cago: University of Chicago Press, 1999).
    6. Robert A. Margo, "Wages and Labor Markets before the Civil War,"
American Economic Review, Papers and Proceedings 88 (May 1998): 53.
    7. Douglass C. North, *The Economic Growth of the United States, 1790–
1960* (Englewood Cliffs, NJ: Prentice-Hall, 1961), 122.
    8. Robert F. Hoxie, "Adequacy of the Customs Revenue System,"
Journal of Political Economy 3 (December 1894): 55.
    9. Frank W. Taussig, "The Tariff, 1830–1860," *Quarterly Journal of
Economics* 2 (April 1888): 324n.
    10. Robert B. Ekelund Jr. and Robert D. Tollison, *Politicized Econo-
mies: Monarchy, Monopoly, and Mercantilism* (College Station: Texas A&M
University Press, 1997).
    11. Paul A. David, "Learning by Doing and Tariff Protection: A Re-
consideration of the Case of the Ante-Bellum United States Cotton Textile Industry," *Journal of Economic History* 30 (September 1970): 521–601.

12. Jonathan J. Pincus, "Pressure Groups and the Pattern of Tariffs," *Journal of Political Economy* 83 (1975): 757–78; idem, *Pressure Groups and Politics in Antebellum Tariffs* (New York: Columbia University Press, 1977).

13. Pincus, "Pressure Groups and the Pattern of Tariffs," 769.

14. Pincus, *Pressure Groups and Politics in Antebellum Tariffs*, 62–63.

15. George J. Stigler, "The Theory of Economic Regulation," *Bell Journal of Economics and Management Science* 2 (Spring 1971): 3–21; Sam Peltzman, "Toward a More General Theory of Regulation," *Journal of Law and Economics* 19 (August 1976): 211–40.

16. Frank W. Taussig, *The Tariff History of the United States* (New York: G. P. Putnam's Sons, 1888), 73.

17. Robert A. McGuire and T. Norman van Cott, "The Confederate Constitution, Tariffs, and the Laffer Relationship," *Economic Inquiry* 40 (July 2002): 428–38.

18. Gerald Gunderson, "The Origins of the American Civil War," *Journal of Economic History* 34 (December 1974): 917.

19. Ibid., 933.

20. Samuel Rezneck, "The Influence of Depression upon American Opinion, 1857–1859," *Journal of Economic History* 2 (May 1942): 1–23; Arthur H. Cole, "Statistical Background of the Crisis of 1857," *Review of Economic Statistics* 12 (November 1930): 170–80.

CHAPTER TWO

THE UNION BLOCKADE AND SOUTHERN STRATEGY

[Had blockade-running been] encouraged, instead of
having obstacles thrown in the way, I am convinced
that the conditions of affairs would have been altered
very materially, and perhaps would have led to the
South obtaining what it had shed so much blood to
gain, viz., its independence.
—Thomas E. Taylor, *Running the Blockade* (1896)

A CRITICAL ELEMENT OF Union strategy was an attempt to reduce
the international trade of the South. General Winfield Scott, de-
signer of the Anaconda Plan that would purportedly engulf the
Confederacy like a snake, reasoned correctly that an effective
blockade would severely injure the Southern war effort. On
April 19, 1861, President Abraham Lincoln proclaimed a blockade on the ports of South Carolina, Alabama, Florida, Mississippi,
Louisiana, and Texas. The blockade was extended to North Carolina ports a week later. At first, international trade and coastal
shipping were conducted as usual, but in late 1861 and in 1862
the blockade began to bring about shortages and higher prices in
vital goods and materials.

Lincoln's proclamation had a number of important effects.
The blockade created new profit potential for blockade-runners.
An active and vital entrepôt trade developed between England
and the Confederacy. Munitions, ordnance, and other military
supplies along with goods destined for Southern civilians passed
through the ports of Bermuda and the Bahamas. With the exception of a few Confederate-owned vessels, blockade-running was
carried on by private interests and contractors who shipped combined cargoes of private goods and supplies destined for the Confederate military.[1]

While land battles and military strategy receive the bulk of attention, the most important battlefield of the war was at sea, fought between one side that neither wore military uniforms nor fired weapons (the blockade-runners) and the other side that rarely fired their weapons to destroy their enemy (the blockaders, who were paid based on what they captured), and where the actions of both sides were based almost entirely on the profit motive. Viewed in this light, it is not surprising that economists consider the blockade to be the decisive battlefield of the war.[2]

The economic, political, and social impacts of the Union's Anaconda Plan and the Confederate response are discussed in this chapter. Blockades, as the modern U.S. experience with Cuba and Iraq reveal, are often leaky affairs and are difficult to enforce. How effective was the Union blockade of the South at reducing the supply of imports? Here we consider its impact on the composition of imports into the Confederacy and reach some conclusions concerning the blockade's economic impact on the conduct and conclusion of the war. In contrast to many historical accounts, we focus on the economics of the blockade, on the policies of both North and South, and on the incentives of blockade-runners. These economic policies and incentives were of critical importance in the war's outcome, both in economic and political terms. Of great importance in any discussion, of course, was the Southern response to Lincoln's blockade—the "King Cotton" strategy.

SOUTHERN TRADE, KING COTTON, AND THE CONFEDERATE EMBARGO

The South was highly dependent on cotton agriculture for its economic success. Prior to the war, resources were allocated almost exclusively on the basis of comparative advantage and international trade. The Southern economy had grown rapidly and developed a thriving agriculture with a comparative advantage in cotton. The South was the lowest-cost producing region in the world, the largest producer, and the largest exporter of raw cotton, the commodity that fueled the Industrial Revolution.

According to informed estimates, the value of Southern manufacturing in 1860 was $155 million.[3] The number of manufacturing firms in the South represented 14.7 percent of the national total in 1860 while the value of Southern products represented only 8.2 percent of the total manufacturing value, which suggests smaller scales of production than in the North. The bulk of this amount was manufacturing related to agriculture or locational cost advantages. Gross farm income of the South in 1859 was $575 million, with $277 million in cotton alone. Farm income was therefore almost four times that derived from manufacturing. The likelihood of Confederate independence would obviously have been enhanced by policies designed to make use of the South's comparative advantage. But the reality appears to be that the Southern economy was materially harmed by both the Union blockade and Confederate policies that impeded this advantage.

In *Cotton is King: or Slavery in the Light of Political Economy* (1855), David Christy argued that cotton grown on Southern plantations fueled the Industrial Revolution and was therefore a powerful economic tool in international affairs. "King Cotton" was critical for textile manufacturing in both the North and in England where as many as five million workers were employed in the textile mills. Advocates of the King Cotton thesis thought that an embargo would cause a shortage of cotton in Europe, devastate the European (as well as Northern) textile industry, and thereby draw England and France into the conflict to break the blockade. According to Owsley, "King Cotton became a cardinal principle upon which all the men who were to lead the South out of the Union and to guide its destiny through the Civil War were almost unanimously agreed."[4]

In the early days of the Confederacy, advocates of King Cotton petitioned Congress for cotton embargo legislation. While unsuccessful in obtaining this legislation, Confederate president Jefferson Davis and his administration lent "tacit approval" to the embargo.[5] More direct success was achieved at the state and local levels, where state laws were passed and citizen committees applied extralegal pressure against cotton exports.[6] According to J. G. Randall and David Donald, "The extraordinary difficulty of getting cotton out of Southern ports in 1861 justified the Southern representations abroad that an 'air-tight embargo' on the export of cotton had been put into effect."[7] The decline in cotton exports was dramatic. In the first year of the war, exports of cotton declined by more than 99 percent. According to John

Schwab, "During the season 1860–61 New Orleans exported one and a half million bales of cotton; during the following season the amount fell to 11,000. The total exports of Southern cotton during the same time fell from two millions of bales to 13,000."[8] These wartime numbers are "official" figures, which are probably much less than the actual exports due to chaotic conditions, evasion of the cotton tax, and other restrictions. Meanwhile, production of cotton remained high early in the war with almost four million bales produced in 1861. With the cotton trade at a standstill, the growing threat of an effective blockade was virtually ignored.[9]

The Confederate Congress and administration's deliberations and contemplation of a cotton embargo tended to support the de facto embargo. Unfortunately for the Confederates, such considerations had a negative effect on their overall foreign policy by creating the impression in Europe that King Cotton was nothing but a paper monarch because cotton was still largely available on the Continent. Early in the war, England drew down its inventory of cotton, faced a drop in demand for its cotton goods, and suffered from a shortfall of wheat production (which it imported from the North). As the war progressed, labor shifted from cotton textiles to munitions and war goods. The increase in the price of cotton resulted in new sources of supply, such as Egypt and India. Concurrently, the lack of cotton imports from the South helped provide evidence that Lincoln's "paper" blockade was effective in cutting off trade and therefore was a legal and binding blockade. In other words, the South would probably have done better if the Confederacy had either strictly enforced a comprehensive embargo or had aggressively exported cotton. A comprehensive embargo might have effectively threatened European textile interests while a policy of aggressive exports would have provided clear evidence that the Union had imposed an illegal paper blockade. Either policy would have increased the possibility of European intervention early in the war.

THE UNION BLOCKADE: THE SETTING

An enormous and rich literature exists on the many economic aspects of the Civil War. While numerous features of the Southern economy are important with respect to the blockade, we focus on the relative prices and composition of imports. As with all wars, tremendous pressures were placed on markets to provide for the civilian population as well as for the war effort. Mobilization in the South—given the highly specialized agrarian nature of the economy—presented profound difficulties.[10] Prior to the war, a large portion of Southern agricultural production was devoted to exports of cotton and tobacco, as mentioned above. Virtually all accounts suggest that most markets for foodstuffs, farm implements, and machinery to produce goods of all kinds were in grave disarray. The shift from comparative advantage to the production of the domestic food supply and other goods—both voluntary and mandated—was often difficult and sometimes unsuccessful.[11]

Most historians also blame the severity and extent of market dislocations on the monetary policy of the Confederate government.[12] Unable to impose taxes to finance the war, the Davis administration followed the timeworn practice of currency depreciation. Calculations by the leading authority on Civil War prices show an eleven fold increase in the money stock over the three years from January 1861 to January 1864 in the South.[13] Between October 1861 and March 1864 the general price index of the Confederacy rose at a rate of 10 percent per month, causing the general price index to rise to ninety-two times its prewar base.[14]

Defeat was perhaps inherent in this method of redistributive finance, but Confederate inflation is only a partial explanation for higher prices. The increase in the price level in the Confederacy was also the result of a rapid rise in the velocity of circulation of money, a decline in real output, and price speculation. Institutional changes and the economic incentives brought on by the actual and anticipated inflation tax provide a strong ground for explaining the process of Southern inflation and critical market dislocations. Speculation, hoarding, and all manner of fraud accompanied and helped generate these dislocations and fanned the fires of inflation. Legal attempts to stem speculation forced domestic and imported product substitutions, engendered price controls at various times at both state and Confederacy levels, and encouraged government support of certain industries, such as salt, and prohibition of others, such as alcoholic beverages.[15] These policy maneuvers were economic failures and did little to stabilize prices.

The general price level rose unabated. Prices of individual goods, owing to particular elasticity characteristics in markets, did not rise at the same rate. The dismal conditions that came to exist in the South were exacerbated by a number of other factors, however. The Union blockade reduced trade, production, and income in general, but one important (and neglected) factor was the influence of the blockade on the price and resource structure in the South. As we will see, the blockade had an influence on *relative prices* within the Confederacy and, even more important, on relative shortages of goods and services. These shortages had a material effect on the course of the war since, in principle, shortages could have been alleviated and the war effort strengthened with the importation of goods and armaments from Europe and elsewhere.

Lincoln's invocation of the blockade had several immediate impacts. There were the usual "announcement effects" in markets where shortages were expected. Speculation and hoarding caused prices to rise in advance of the initial currency depreciation by the Confederates in these markets. And, as we have already mentioned, new profit opportunities opened up for blockade-runners and for English traders. Military supplies of all kinds together with items destined for Southern civilians were routed through Bermuda and the Bahamas. These largely private adventurers carried all goods to the Confederacy. And run they did. Marcus Price reports that during 1861, the first year of Lincoln's blockade, twenty-one steamers and 253 sailing vessels were attempting to run the Yankee blockade of the Carolina coast.[16]

Another immediate impact of the Union blockade was to spur the deployment and development of steam-powered vessels, which, by 1861, were effectively competing with sail power. Common economic sense tells us why. Most sailing vessels, including schooners, brigantines, ships, barques, sloops, and yachts, were not (at least initially) economic matches for steam-powered Union ships deployed to blockade the South. While schooners could, under appropriate conditions, outrun steam blockade ships, they were often of insufficient cargo-carrying capacity to make most runs lucrative, although such ships were employed as blockade-runners throughout the war. Larger sailing ships were of insufficient speed, and all of them were sitting ducks if they lost their wind power. Steam vessels of light draft (especially for the shallow Gulf of Mexico), speed, and capacity were the most desirable. Economic incentives encouraged the production and use of larger numbers of them for blockade-running, and eventually ships specifically designed to run through the blockade were designed and built.

UNION CAPTURE RATES

How effective was the Union blockade of the South in reducing the supply of all imports? Moreover, how important was the blockade in changing the relative prices and compositions of imports to Southerners? In order to answer these questions, we focus on the supply of and demand for these commodities during the Civil War in the South. First, consider the impact of the blockade on the suppliers of these imports. A major cost of supplying all imports, both "luxuries" and "necessities," to the South was the possibility (or probability) of capture for blockade-runners. Thus, an assessment of the size and levels of constant per unit costs to suppliers of Southern imports requires an accurate estimate of *inbound* capture rates.

The capture rate of incoming vessels is an approximate measure of supply costs, but the actual supply was influenced by a number of factors. Capture rates will clearly underestimate the supply reduction of Southern imports and the strength of the prohibition on relative import prices. As Donald McCloskey explained, the imposition of a prohibition or a blockade affects the cost and supply curves of traders in two ways; first, the higher actual costs (investments in faster and smaller vessels) to shippers; and second, the variability of a successful yield (as distinct from a lower average yield) from the threat of seizure must be included in their cost calculations in the same manner that ordinary shippers include insurance in their accounting of explicit costs. Actual capture rates therefore underestimate supply reductions in the sense that they do not reflect the quantities of goods that would have been transported in the absence of the chance of seizure.[17] Fortunately, excellent data on inbound and outbound capture rates exist from two sources. Marcus Price provided the most complete account of coastal blockade-running in all types of vessels.[18] Using this data, we calculate the capture rate as the percentage of unsuccessful attempts to total attempts to run the Union blockade. As the blockade took hold, capture rates of sailing vessels rose dramatically around all ports—Gulf, Georgia and East Florida, and the Carolinas. Aggregate capture rates for steam vessels, however, rose sharply between 1861 and 1862, but either remained fairly constant or declined between 1862 and 1865. Overall rates for both inbound and outbound captures rose sharply between 1861 and 1862, stabilized at approximately 35 percent for 1862 and 1863, rose to 39 percent in 1864, and declined to 22 percent as the war ended in the first five months of 1865. These aggregate capture rates are depicted in Figure 2-1.

Price's evidence is broadly corroborated by more recent data provided by Stephen Wise on blockade-running by steam-powered vessels only. His data on inbound rates follow the same pattern as the capture rates for all voyages—a sharp rise in capture rates between 1861 and 1862, followed by declining rates in 1863 and 1864, although the rate does increase in 1865.[19]

THE BLOCKADE AND RELATIVE IMPORT PRICES

Blockades increase the domestic supply of previously exported goods, with price-lowering effects. They also decrease the domestic supply of goods formerly imported, with price-increasing effects. The Union blockade of the South was not different. In terms of specific commodities, the South exclusively imported such items as wool, coffee, tea, and salt. Southerners relied heavily on imports of cotton rope, sheeting, shirting, cotton yarn, wool yarn, iron, cut nails, and shoe soles and uppers. Attempts at import substitution were common. Salt, for example, was extremely scarce and was the subject of conservation, local production, and attempted substitutions. In addition to sugar (prior to the early Federal capture of New Orleans in 1862), rock salt was also supplied from Louisiana, and the Confederate government attempted to generate domestic salt production in Alabama and Virginia. These attempts met with very limited success, however, due to speculation and to the chicanery of government contractors.

Economist Eugene Lerner has demonstrated that price increases from highest to lowest in magnitude occurred for imports (as defined above), partially imported goods, domestically

Figure 2-1. Blockade Capture Rates, 1861–1865

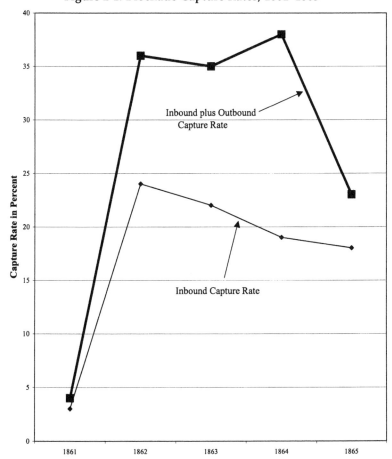

Sources: Marcus W. Price, "Ships that Tested the Blockade of the Carolina Ports, 1861–1865," *American Neptune* 8 (1948): 215–38; idem, "Ships that Tested the Blockade of the Gulf Ports, 1861–1865," *American Neptune* 11 (1951): 279–90 and 12 (1952): 154–61, 229–36; idem, "Ships that Tested the Blockade of the Georgian and East Florida Ports, 1861–1865," *American Neptune* 15 (1955): 97–132.

produced goods, and exports. All manner of high-priced goods were carried into the South, including (virtually all) medicines and such items as dresses, cognac, cordials, ribbon, gloves, hoop skirts, spices, and furniture. Observers at the time noted the continued availability and sale of high-price, low-bulk imports after the war began while basic necessities were in tight supply. Mary Elizabeth Massey provides an assessment of imports that came through the blockade: "the shortage of such items as boiler iron, steel, copper, zinc, and machinery of all kinds was not relieved to any great extent by blockade-running. Such things as quinine, morphine, expensive dress materials, laces, and miscellaneous items were brought in greater quantity. The majority of articles brought by private runners were luxuries, while articles of great necessity came in slight quantity or not at all."[20] Wise notes that the steamship *Acadia*, bound for Texas through Bermuda, carried all manner of speculative household supplies, including porcelain toilets "complete with a lead base and a brass flusher designed by Thomas Crapper."[21] According to the testimony of a real-life Rhett Butler, famous blockade-runner Thomas Taylor, "the chief requirements were war materials of every sort, cloth for uniforms, buttons, thread, boots, stockings, and all clothing, medicines, salt, boiler-iron, steel, copper, zinc, and chemicals. As it did not pay merchants to ship heavy goods, the charge for freight per ton at Nassau being £80 to £100 in gold, a great portion of the cargo generally consisted of light goods, such as silks, laces, linens, quinine, etc., on which immense profits were made."[22] Massey herself reports that choice wines, brandies, and whiskies were brought through the blockade and were purchased immediately, despite their exorbitant cost.[23]

The examples seem endless: bonnet ribbon, playing cards, corset stays (reputedly brought through the blockade at an 1,100 percent profit), sewing needles, all kinds of personal items, children's dolls, musical instruments, spices, and pepper were all in the active runner's trade. President Davis, who was furious over such transactions and the profiteering that accompanied them, urged and achieved congressional passage of an act forbidding such importation on February 6, 1864.[24] The law was of little avail, however, and luxuries continued to be smuggled into the South.

Historians have long puzzled over this phenomenon of luxury imports. Lerner, for example, argues that "the reason why blockade-runners carried 'Yankee geegaws, silks and trinkets' rather than necessities" was that "the price of wheat, corn, and other products produced in limited quantities in the Confederacy simply did not rise fast enough."[25] While the effects of demand and supply on prices are clearly relevant to the explanation, we must look to factors affecting demand and supply during the war in order to explain why "luxuries" kept flowing into the Confederacy. In short, we must look to factors affecting import suppliers over the period of the blockade. One of the new factors during the war was the risk of getting caught running the blockade, and it is this risk-adjusted cost that helps explain the composition of goods imported into the South during the Civil War.

THE ECONOMIC THEORY OF THE RHETT BUTLER EFFECT

Most beginning students of economics are warned that the identification of "luxury" or "necessity" goods in terms of differences in nominal prices is artificial and indirect. Imported "luxuries," such as ladies' bonnets, lace, wines, spices, medicines, and coffee, were goods of high value in proportion to weight and/or volume. Imported "necessities," such as salt, sugar, molasses, or metals, were, in many cases, items of low value in proportion to bulk (weight and/or volume), hereafter the VB ratio. Further, purely for linguistic convenience, we identify goods with high VB ratios as luxuries and those with low VB ratios as necessities. As we have mentioned elsewhere in this chapter, the Confederate government placed severe space limitations on blockade-runners late in the war, but there was always wide latitude in the selection of goods transported until the prohibition of "luxuries" as the war was drawing to an end.[26]

A concept of a "risk-adjusted cost" to suppliers may be expressed simply. Assume that a "representative" imported luxury item or bundle of items with price P_l and imported necessities with price P_n can be identified in a simplified model of market functioning. Although diverse in nature, these goods are related as imports in the same manner as different qualities of a single good. Costs of supplying these goods were initially composed of resource and transportation costs, C. Under competitive conditions, prices tend to equal costs. A blockade adds another element—a constant per-unit cost associated with the risk of running the blockade. This risk cost is independent of the nature of the cargo transported. The blockade-runner measures the probability of being caught, the loss of the ship and cargo, and the possibilities of capture, imprisonment, or death. With all other factors equal, the probability of a successful run decreases as more resources are devoted to blockade enforcement. Total cost (including risk) equals C_r, and prior to the blockade, the risk cost, aside from the ordinary risks of shipping, is zero. If, initially, the ratio of P_l/P_n is equal to some value Z, then $(P_l + C_r)/(P_n + C_r)$ is less than Z. As the blockade tightens, C_r rises and the value of the risk cost-adjusted ratio becomes smaller. Essentially, luxuries become cheaper to import relative to necessities. During the Civil War, this fact affected the incentives to blockade-runners and therefore the relative quantities of different types of goods that were sent through the blockade and into Southern markets. This impact of the blockade we have dubbed the Rhett Butler Effect because, like the fictional character in *Gone With the Wind*, economic incentives encouraged runners to import luxury goods.

For example, suppose that one pound of coffee or two pounds of sugar may be purchased in Charleston for one dollar. If the blockade increases the transport cost between Bermuda and Charleston by one dollar per pound, then one pound of coffee in Charleston will cost the same as one and one-third pounds of sugar. If the transport cost increases by two dollars per pound, one pound of coffee will cost the same as one and one-fifth pounds of sugar. The risks of the blockade make sugar relatively more expensive to run than coffee. Therefore, the blockade will increase the price of both goods, but it will reduce the *relative price* of coffee.

Blockades therefore raise prices of all imports by equal absolute amounts (due to the new risk cost that suppliers have to incorporate), but they distort relative costs and incentives to suppliers. The relative costs (including risk) of supplying items with high VB ratios to Southern consumers declined vis-à-vis those with low ratios as the blockade increased in effectiveness. Southern demanders therefore faced lower relative prices for imports with high VB ratios in contrast to the other kinds of imports under blockade conditions. Relative prices shifted to purchasers due to the relative quantities of imports supplied to the Southern market. An increased relative supply of luxury goods had a price-depressing effect while a reduced supply of necessities increased prices. As the Federal blockade tightened, the relative price of luxury imports fell versus all other imports within the South. This overall economic effect of the blockade is depicted graphically in Figure 2-2.

Figure 2-2. Consumption Possibilities and the Blockade

Quantity of Luxuries

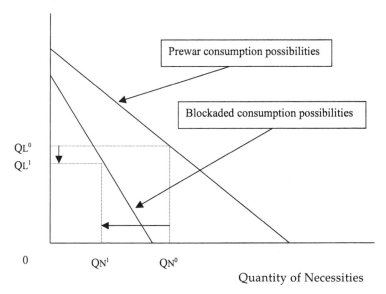

In Figure 2-2 both pre- and post-blockade consumption possibilities are depicted. The people of the Southern economy could consume any combination of luxuries and necessities along the consumption possibility curves. Along the prewar curve, the economy chose equal amounts of luxuries and necessities. After the war started and the blockade was imposed, the consumption possibility curve shifts inward toward the origin of the graph. It also rotates toward the vertical axis indicating that necessities have risen in price relative to luxuries. Given these possibilities, the economy will choose to consume a lesser quantity of both luxuries and necessities, but it will choose to consume more luxuries relative to necessities.

This model does not require a priori or intertemporal constraints on the identities of particular products as "necessities" or "luxuries." Indeed, product switching is an implication of the model. Since inbound supplies will depend partly on initial relative price differences and since supplies will have relative price-depressing and price-elevating effects over time, "switching" between luxuries and necessities would be possible over the longer run. In other words, the necessities of one time could conceivably become the luxuries of another with a large-enough change in relative prices caused by blockade-created supply decreases. These value changes would naturally and in time have a reaction on the incentives of blockade-runners. It appears that a negative relation between the severity of the blockade and the ratio of "luxury" prices to "necessity" prices would be expected within the time frame of the Union blockade. However, it is unlikely that the blockade period—roughly forty-six months—was long enough to create much switching.

THE UNION BLOCKADE AND
RELATIVE PRICES: EVIDENCE

Consistent and continuous data on the prices and quantities traded of Yankee and European "geegaws" are unavailable between 1861 and 1865. However, sporadic and incidental notations in journals, diaries, and newspaper reports strongly support the notion that imported luxuries of all kinds were flowing through the blockade. In addition, it is possible to construct a continuous data series of certain commodity prices over the war years from newspaper sources and quotations. Indeed, excellent price series of this type were compiled and collected at the turn of the century.[27] In addition to John Schwab's research, which charted indices for twenty-two commodities, more recent data series also provide a basis for an informal evaluation of the idea that a relative price change created a higher proportion of luxury imports into the South.[28]

Since speculation and hoarding were rampant—at times spurred on by official price controls and import restrictions—it is virtually impossible to obtain consistent and comparable records of transacted (retail) prices for any good or commodity. Therefore, while an accurate tabulation of transacted retail price series may be more desirable for many purposes, they do not exist. Wholesale price series generated from newspaper quotations are more uniform and homogeneous and are systematically reported. In addition, major import commodities—coffee, tea, molasses, sugar, salt, and finished nails—are included in newspaper compilations.

As a first approximation, consider the annual ratio of the sum of coffee and tea prices (considered "luxuries") to the sum of sugar and molasses prices between 1861 and 1865. Coffee and, to a lesser extent, tea were considered luxury goods over the war years.[29] Massey reports that Atlanta jewelers set coffee beans instead of diamonds in breast pins.[30] Further, there was a significant difference in relative prices between coffee and sugar. The base price of coffee to sugar per pound prior to the opening of hostilities, for example, was greater than 2 to 1 in Richmond as it was in Montgomery, Alabama, and Augusta, Georgia.[31] Sugar and molasses were also very scarce. Louisiana supplied a portion of the total sugar demand to the Confederacy until 1862 (when Union forces took control of New Orleans), after which the entire supply of sugar was imported.

The Rhett Butler Effect implies that as the blockade became more severe and the relative costs of blockade-runners adjusted to the constraint, the price of luxuries relative to necessities fell within the South. The evidence, using annual data, conforms nicely to this hypothesis. Figure 2-3, utilizing the index data computed by Schwab, shows a rising ratio of the relatively higher-priced (low bulk) coffee and tea to the relatively lower-priced (higher bulk) sugar and molasses between 1861 and 1862. As the blockade became more effective (in terms of inbound capture rates), the *relative price* of these two classes of imported commodities fell from 1862 through 1864 owing, in large measure, to relative wartime supply shifts within the South. The dramatic rise over the first months of 1865 coincides with the generally lower capture rates in all ports, that is, an easing of the blockade prohibition (see Figure 2-1), and with the intense attempts to utilize substitutes for coffee and all other imports in an avoidance of the blockade.

Schwab's data also permits a quarterly calculation of the ratio of coffee to sugar and molasses prices from the first quarter of

Figure 2-3. Ratio of Luxury Prices to Necessity Prices

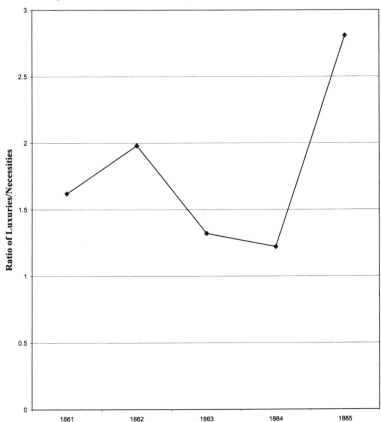

Source: John C. Schwab, "Prices in the Confederate States, 1861–1865," *Political Science Quarterly* (June 1899): 281–83. Here luxuries are tea and coffee and necessities are represented by molasses and sugar.

1861 through the first quarter of 1865 (Figure 2-4) in both the Confederacy and the United States. (Quarterly data on tea prices are incomplete and unusable.) These data show that the dramatic rise in the ratio occurred between the first two quarters of 1861 and the last two quarters of that year (the average rose from 1.015

to 3.047). As the blockade began to take effect in 1862, the ratio of prices systematically declined until the first quarter of 1865 in the Confederacy. The calculated trend line of the price ratio for the Confederacy between the first quarter of 1862 (the beginning

Figure 2-4. Price Ratio of Coffee to Sugar and Molasses

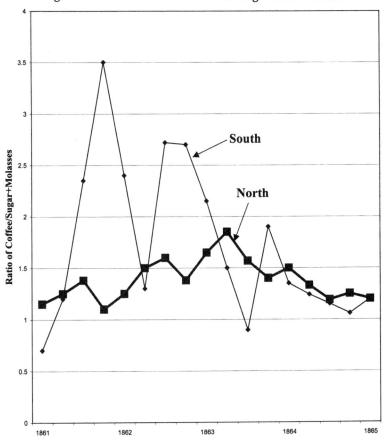

Source: John C. Schwab, "Prices in the Confederate States, 1861–1865," *Political Science Quarterly* (June 1899): 295.

of effective blockade) and the first quarter of 1865 is negative (-0.057) and significant at the 15 percent level (T-statistic = -1.5718). The trend line for the Union ratio is positive but not significant at any acceptable level. While relative prices were rising in the

North, they fell in the South in spite of worldwide production shortfalls of coffee between 1861 and 1865.[32] Data on quantities traded are extremely scarce. What do exist are difficult to arrange in a systematic fashion. Cargo manifests of runners departing St. George, Bermuda, with critical qualifications and caveats attached to the sample, provide some indication of relative supply. Table 2-2 shows the quantities of coffee, tea, and sugar transshipped from Bermuda between April 22, 1862, and February 24, 1865. Despite the difficulties aggregating diverse units of measurement, it is clear that coffee and tea were favorite objects of transport for the blockade-runner. Coffee (and tea, which was apparently imported in increased amounts in 1864) was brought in throughout the war, although it is not possible to differentiate between that destined for private consumption and that devoted to Confederate Army uses. Molasses importation was practically nonexistent in the sample (five barrels in 1863), and sugar imports (also in rationed use by the Army) did not undergo any dramatic rise relative to coffee and tea. It is known that by 1862, Army rations excluded coffee; and that by December 10, 1863, the Surgeon General ordered that it not be used as food for the sick but only as a stimulant for medicinal purposes.[33] Coffee and tea continued to arrive, moreover, in spite of the fact that the Confederate government tried to regulate the contents of inbound and outbound vessels carried on private account.[34]

While aggregate price index observations and risk rates (proxied by capture data), along with a very small sample of cargo shipped, conform well with the Rhett Butler Effect, there was obviously much variation in price behavior in the cities and regions of the Confederacy. Relative scarcities of all commodities, imported and domestic, varied between Texas and Carolina cities and between the Eastern and Western Confederacy depending in large part on the success of the blockade. The port city of Wilmington, North Carolina, for instance, continued to receive massive quantities of goods and supplies and was relatively unencumbered by the blockade until war's end. A regional check of relative prices of coffee to those of sugar and molasses, with data collected and compiled from the cities of Augusta and Montgomery for selected dates between 1861 and 1865, yields observations similar to those of aggregate Southern price data. The Augusta monthly ratio peaked in December 1861, fell dramatically until July 1862, rose through December 1862, and declined thereafter. Substitution might have been a factor since tea was available and rising in price over part of the period (between March and July 1862), but such substitution was limited. Although data for Montgomery are less complete, price experience closely followed the pattern of Augusta. Price ratios for Richmond, Virginia, are less volatile but reveal a significantly declining trend from 1862 to 1864.[35]

Table 2-2. Inbound Commodity Shipments from St. George, Bermuda, from Cargo Manifests, 1862–1865

Year	Coffee		Tea		Sugar	
1862	146	Bags	114.5	Chests	6	Barrels
(2 vessels)	10	Bags	5	Cases		
1863	1,015	Bags	90	Chests	141	Barrels
(15 vessels)			50	Caddies	2	Hogsheads
			17	Boxes	10	Tierces
			100	Cases		
1864	105	Bags	110	Chests	406	Barrels
(23 vessels)	21	Barrels	356	Cases	2	Boxes
					5	Hogsheads
					4	Tierces
1865	2,459	Bags	295	Chests	12	Barrels
(6 vessels)						

Source: Frank Vandiver, *Confederate Blockade Running through Bermuda, 1861–1865: Letters and Cargo Manifests* (Austin: University of Texas Press, 1947), 109–48. Reprinted by permission of Frank Vandiver.

A *CONFEDERATE* BLOCKADE OF THE SOUTHERN ECONOMY

The adverse effects of the Union blockade on the amount and kinds of supplies getting to the Confederacy over the war years were debilitating for both citizens and the war effort. Southern policies, to a very large extent, actually made a bad situation worse. First, there was the matter of "impressments," which are forced sales of goods from owners in the private sector to the government. The Confederate policy of impressing goods for the military at below market prices created bitter feelings toward the government on the part of those who were adversely affected.

Those lower prices also resulted in a decreased total supply of provisions because lower prices mean lower quantities supplied. In the short run, for example, farmers would be less inclined to bring their produce to market (hoarding), and in the longer run they would be unwilling to grow as much. The lower prices would also cause hoarding by the military and lead to wastefulness because quartermasters could buy at below market prices. In some locations the policy regressed into mere robbery. And yet when some historians turn their attention to naval policy, impressment of ships is often viewed as a necessary and generally beneficial aspect of the war effort, while the accompanying deleterious effects are ignored.

According to economic theory, a policy of impressment would decrease the supply of ships for either naval or commercial purposes. Impressment typically wastes resources because government officials are able to consume resources at below market prices and/or to allocate these resources to lower valued uses. (In many cases, for example, impressed ships were quickly and unnecessarily destroyed, captured, or put to unproductive uses). Combined with the faulty cotton embargo, the impressment of ships in Southern ports greatly curtailed the South's intranational and international trade at a time when the blockade was ineffective and, therefore, when European goods such as marine engines, railroad machinery, rifled cannons, and repeating rifles could have been imported at prices much lower than later in the war. These and all other imported goods became more expensive as the war continued because of the increased costs associated with blockade-running.[36]

After ships of foreign ownership had departed Southern harbors in 1861, there were only ten oceangoing steamers in the Confederacy. According to Wise, "Southerners were reluctant to put their vessels to use."[37] In fact, several of these steamers were immediately seized or impressed by the government and all of them would "eventually be taken over by the Confederate Navy."[38] The very ships that could have helped defeat the paper blockade of 1861 were seized by the Confederate Army and Navy and by state governments. Government seizure or impressment not only prevented the use of these steamers for profitable purposes but also established a precedent that posed a threat to future private suppliers of steamers.

In addition, the impressed ships were, in general, not very effectively used by the military. Two of the largest and newest steamers were seized by the Virginia Navy and turned over to the Confederate Navy. The *Jamestown*, renamed the *Thomas Jefferson*, was sunk as an obstruction in the James River, while the *Yorktown*, built in 1859, became the home of the Confederate Naval Academy. The largest available steamer, the *Nashville*, was seized at the start of the war for the Confederate Navy, but it only contributed to the war effort after it was sold to private interests in 1862.

Although the policies of the Confederate government might have been well-intentioned, they also contained the seeds of self-destruction. As the war progressed and the Union blockade tightened, the protectionist and interventionist tide continued to swell. Both state and Confederate governments entered the blockade-running business. The Confederacy operated four steamers out of Wilmington to run the blockade with cotton and return with arms, munitions, and provisions. Governor Zebulon B. Vance of North Carolina established a state-run, blockade-running operation in 1862. The states of Georgia and South Carolina entered into joint ventures to reap the profits of blockade-running and, in part, to exempt local firms from the onerous requirement that blockade-runners set aside 50 percent of cargo space for use by the Confederate government.

This division of authority revealed larger problems in the inefficiency in decision making and information dissemination in the Confederacy. A bizarre example is instructive. Heated political debates between President Davis of the Confederacy and the governors of the states often occurred. A dispute regarding the blockade underlines the type of incentive conflicts involved in the states' rights crisis. Indeed, the case of the ship *Little Ada* is a prime example of the conflict of interests or incentives that existed in policy, or what has been called "the partial blockade of our own Executive" (Jefferson Davis). Governor Joseph Emerson Brown of Georgia refused to allow the Confederates space on the *Little Ada*, and President Davis refused the ship clearance to run

the blockade. During the ensuing political squabble the presence
of the ship was reported to Union blockaders, who in a surprise
raid captured the *Little Ada* in port but were ironically denied
their prize by the Confederates, who were blockading *in* the *Little
Ada*. Blockade-runners as a group lost money in the squabbles
between the president and the governors; many also lost the incentive to run the blockade.

Luxury goods, as we have seen, continued to enter the South.
However, partially in response to some vocal public dissatisfac-
tion over the import of luxury goods, legislation was passed in
February 1864 by the Confederate Congress that forbade the import of a large class of luxury goods and placed price controls on
others. The list of prohibited goods was a long one.[39]

Absynthe
Ale, beer, and porter
Anchovies, sardines, and all other fish preserved in oil
Articles embroidered with gold, silver or other metal
Bay rum
Billiard and bagatelle tables, and all other tables or boards
    on which games are played
Brandy and other spirits distilled from grain or other
    materials
Cabinet and household furniture
Carpets, carpeting, hearth-rugs, bed-sides, and tapestry of
    every kind and description
Carriages, and parts of carriages
Cotton laces
Diamonds, cameos, mosaics, gems, pearls, rubies, and other
    precious stones, and imitations thereof, when set in
    gold, silver or other metal, and when not set
Dolls and toys of all kinds
Glass, cut; Glass, colored, stained or painted
Leaf and manufactured tobacco and cigars
Manufactures and articles of marble, marble paving-tiles,
    slabs or block, and all other marble
Muffs and tippets, and all other manufactures of fur, or
    of which fur shall be a component part, except caps
    and hats

THE UNION BLOCKADE AND SOUTHERN STRATEGY   51

Paintings and statuary
Paper hangings; Paper for walls; Paper for screens or
    fireboards
Paving and roofing tiles and bricks, and roofing slates, and
    fire bricks
Perfumes and perfumery of all sorts
Playing cards
Scagliola table-tops, or other articles of furniture
Thread lacings and insertings; Velvets of all kinds
Wines, burgundy, champagne, claret, madeira, port, sherry,
    and all other wines and imitations of wines

This prohibition, which is generally viewed as a policy that was too little and too late in regulating the blockade-runners, had a doubly negative impact on the war effort. First, luxury goods had high value relative to bulk and therefore contributed greatly to profits and in many cases to the spirit of the crews. Many of the captains, officers, and crewmen of blockade-runners were allowed to bring in a small amount of goods on their own account in order to enhance their pay and the prospects of a successful voyage. They almost always chose luxury goods that gave them the greatest return. Second, the Act of February 1864 prohibited beer, spirits, and wine, which, combined with state prohibitions on alcoholic beverages, created an extreme scarcity. Spirits had traditionally served as a highly compact and transportable source of calories for sailors and soldiers as well as an indispensable medical commodity.

Most states had passed prohibitory laws during 1862 and as a result "the price of whiskey jumped skyward."[40] The War Department used considerable amounts of whiskey in hospitals and in concocting medicines.[41] Furthermore, whiskey was a practical substitute or supplement for bread and in fact surpassed bread in being a more durable, transportable, and versatile grain product, especially under battlefield conditions. Alcohol was also a regular component of a sailor's rations, as recommended by the Surgeon General. General Joseph E. Johnston, for example, decided that whiskey might make up for deficiencies in the meat rations of his men. However, the regular issue of whiskey had to be suspended in 1863 because of a short supply. According to Joseph T.

Durkin, Secretary of the Navy Stephen R. Mallory tried to establish a distillery in South Carolina to produce whiskey for Navy use.[42] It appears that the South was better off because of the laxness and difficulty of enforcing state legislation on trade. The Confederate Congress also authorized the Treasury Department to regulate the export of cotton, tobacco, military and naval stores, rice, and sugar in February 1864. Shortly thereafter it required that one-half of the outgoing and incoming cargo space be reserved for the Confederate government. This legislation had a direct and visible impact on blockade-running and the economic viability of the South. Good data on blockade attempts through Carolina ports in 1863 and 1864 carried the presumption that attempted runs sharply diminished between these two years (from 515 in 1863 to 387 in 1864).[43] The number of runs through the blockade at Wilmington by steam-powered ships was about the same during the year before the legislation as the year afterward. Given that most other ports were occupied or effectively blockaded in 1864 and 1865 and that a number of new private and public steamers had come on line in 1864, we would have expected blockade-running into Wilmington to have substantially increased, which it did not.

To top off all of this self-defeating regulation, the Act of February 1864 further instructed the Confederate Secretary of the Treasury, C. G. Memminger, to place strict price controls on "goods manufactured wholly or partly of cotton, flax, wool, or of silk, and designed for wearing apparel."[44] The following is a sample:

(Cotton) Drawers, ready made, knit or woven, not to exceed
    $1 per pair;
(Cotton) Gloves, not to exceed 25 cents per pair;
(Cotton) Hosiery, women's, not to exceed 35 cents per pair;
(Cotton) Shirts, ready made, knit or woven, not to exceed
    $1 each;
(Wool) Hats, men's, not to exceed $2 each;
(Wool) Hats, women's, not to exceed $4 each;
(Wool) Shawls, not to exceed $7.50 each;
Dress Silk, not to exceed $1 per yard;
Sewing Silk, not to exceed $5 per yard.

Clearly, such price controls created shortages if, as was likely, legal prices were set below market-determined prices. As Stanley Lebergott has shown, the business of blockade-running was difficult on its own, so that foreign suppliers, let alone blockade-runners, were far less willing to send these items to the Confederacy after controlled prices were enforced.[45] The suppression of prices and profits, no matter what the motive, likely had deleterious effects on Southerners and the Confederate war effort.

"RHETT BUTLER" AND OTHER RUNNERS SPEAK

Shortly after the various features of the 1864 legislation were put into effect, Captain Roberts, one of the most successful blockade-runners, ceased all activities, saying:

> The game, indeed, was fast drawing to a close. Its decline was caused in the first instance by the impolitic behaviour of the people at Wilmington, who, professedly acting under orders from the Confederate Government at Richmond, pressed the blockade-runners into their service to carry out cotton on Government account in such an arbitrary manner, that the profit to their owners, who had been put to an enormous expense and risk in sending vessels in, was so much reduced that the ventures hardly paid.[46]

Another of the most famous and successful blockade-runners —often believed to have been the real-life model for Margaret Mitchell's character of Rhett Butler in *Gone With the Wind*—was Thomas Taylor, who made twenty-eight trips through the blockade. One of Taylor's first recollections in his chronicle of events was the Confederate government's 1864 Act (discussed above) to limit freight on private account and its prohibition on imported luxuries. Unlike Captain Roberts, Taylor continued to run the blockade because he had negotiated a secret profit arrangement with the Confederate Commissary-General that compensated him for the 1864 legislation. Late in the war, despite his best efforts to the contrary, Taylor accurately predicted the downfall of the Confederacy. Writing to his superiors on January 15, 1865, he said, "I never saw things look so gloomy, and I think spring will finish them unless they make a change for the better." As he put it, had blockade-running been encouraged, "instead of having obstacles thrown in the way, I am convinced that the conditions of affairs would have been altered very materially, and perhaps would have led to the South obtaining what it had shed so much blood to gain, viz., its independence."[47]

It appears that blockade-runners could adjust to the advances of the Union blockade, but not to the economic constraints of the Confederate legislation. As Captain Roberts explained, "the enterprise had lost much of its charm; for, unromantic as it may seem, much of that charm consisted in money-making."[48] Economic motives, however much we support or reject them ethically, morally, or philosophically, appear to have determined the outcome for the lifeline of the Confederacy.

It is clear that in order for the Confederacy to achieve independence, it had to survive long enough for the Union government to be defeated politically. Indeed, the election of 1864 might have been such an opportunity. Gary Anderson and Robert Tollison have argued persuasively that "Lincoln sensed that his reelection was in doubt" during the summer of 1864. Only the votes of "loyal" troops prevented the election from going to the peace-oriented Democratic ticket headed by George McClellan, who had been discharged by Lincoln as chief of Union forces.[49] Of lesser note were the elections in Ohio in 1863 where a Peace Democrat victory could have had "dire effects for the cause of the Union" or "might have hampered the state's war effort. Even more important, the peace movement all over the North would have been immeasurably strengthened and Union morale dealt a devastating blow." As Lincoln put it, Ohio had saved the Union.[50] However, survival of the Confederacy depended on policies that would enhance rather than retard the possibilities of successfully waging war against the Union. Many factors might have been employed. In this chapter we have considered only one of them— developing policies toward the blockade and trade that would have enabled it to profit from its economic comparative advantage. In short, the Confederacy failed to employ its economic strength—a free market, cotton-based economy.

The problems faced by the Confederacy in the economic realm were many. First, the King Cotton strategy was a failure. Some cotton was exported from the South through the blockade, but withholding massive cotton inventories at the start of the war did not, as the South had hoped, bring England into the conflict. Not only was the Union blockade responsible for reducing the aggregate supply of imports, but an often neglected effect on relative prices also created an untoward—and ultimately unstoppable—shift in the relative importation of luxuries at the expense of items that might have contributed to the Southern war effort. Evidence is highly suggestive that there was deeper substance to the anecdotes from Southern citizens complaining about the sale of luxury goods and the lack of necessities.

Naturally, the Rhett Butler Effect was no more than one element in the ultimate defeat of the South by the Union. The political inability to produce united policies, the agrarian nature of the Confederacy stemming from prewar Banana Republic-style reliance on cotton and tobacco for revenues, an inadequate transportation system, and numerous other problems were all contributing factors.[51] In the end, the demoralization and defeat of the South may well have been the result of the kind of self-interested economic incentives that were created for blockade-runners and traders of all types described in this chapter. But to go further and label these incentives perverse or corrupting takes us from the realm of objective analysis into normative value judgments. The presence of the Rhett Butler Effect means that, objectively, self-interest will always take a particular direction in response to relative price signals. Economic theory merely predicts that prohibitions or restrictions affecting relative prices will always carry a particular form of incentives. These incentives in turn produce unintended consequences that undermine the goals of those policies. As usual, self-interest proves to be a better predictor of behavior and outcomes than does patriotism or altruism. Admonitions to virtue apparently have far less force when high and rising profits are at stake. Whether or not such effects are "perverse" must be left to the values of the beholder.

NOTES

1. Frank Vandiver, *Confederate Blockade Running through Bermuda, 1861–1865* (Austin: University of Texas Press, 1947), xxxii.
2. David G. Surdam, *Northern Naval Superiority and the Economics of the American Civil War* (Columbia: University of South Carolina Press, 2001).

③ Eugene M. Lerner, "Southern Output and Agricultural Income, 1860–80," *Agriculture History* 33 (July 1959), 117–25, reprinted in *The Economic Impact of the American Civil War*, ed. Ralph Andreano (Cambridge, MA: Schenkman, 1992), 102.

④ David Christy, *Cotton is king: or, The culture of cotton and its relation to agriculture, manufacturers and commerce; to the free colored people; and to those who hold that slavery is in itself sinful; by an American* (Cincinnati: Moore, Wilstach, Keys & Co., 1855); Frank L. Owsley, *King Cotton Diplomacy: Foreign Relations of the Confederate States of America*, 2d ed. (Chicago: University of Chicago Press, [1931] 1959), 15–17.

5. Stephen R. Wise, *Lifeline of the Confederacy: Blockade Running during the Civil War* (Columbia: University of South Carolina Press, 1988), 28.

6. John C. Schwab, *The Confederate States of America, 1861–1865: A Financial History of the South during the Civil War* (New York: Burt Franklin, [1901] 1969), 250–51.

7. J. G. Randall and David Herbert Donald, *The Civil War and Reconstruction*, 2d ed. (Lexington, MA: D. C. Heath and Company, 1969), 501.

8. Schwab, *Confederate States*, 238, 279.

9. Wise, *Lifeline*, 225.

10. Douglass C. North, *Growth and Welfare in the American Past* (Englewood Cliffs, NJ: Prentice-Hall, 1966); idem, *The Economic Growth of the United States, 1790–1860* (Englewood Cliffs, NJ: Prentice-Hall, 1961), 66–74.

11. Charles W. Ramsdell, *Behind the Lines in the Southern Confederacy* (Baton Rouge: Louisiana State University Press, 1944), 88–89.

12. For example, see Andreano, *Economic Impact*.

13. Eugene M. Lerner, "Money, Prices, and Wages in the Confederacy, 1861–1865," *Journal of Political Economy* 63 (February 1955): 21.

14. Ibid., 23–24.

15. William M. Robinson Jr., "Prohibition in the Confederacy," *American Historical Review* 37 (October 1931): 50–58.

16. Marcus W. Price, "Ships that Tested the Blockade of the Carolina Ports, 1861–1865," *American Neptune* 8 (1948): 196.

17. Donald McCloskey, *The Applied Theory of Price*, 2d ed. (New York: Macmillan, 1985), 589.

18. Price, "Ships that Tested the Blockade of the Carolina Ports," 196–241; idem, "Ships that Tested the Blockade of the Gulf Ports, 1861–1865," *American Neptune* 11 (1951): 279–90 and 12 (1952): 52–59, 154–61, 229–38; idem, "Ships that Tested the Blockade of the Georgian and East Florida Ports, 1861–1865," *American Neptune* 15 (1955): 229–38.

19. Wise, *Lifeline*, 233-88.

20. Mary Elizabeth Massey, *Ersatz in the Confederacy* (Columbia: University of South Carolina Press, 1952), 14.

21. Wise, *Lifeline*, 216.

22. Thomas E. Taylor, *Running the Blockade: A Personal Narrative of Adventures, Risks, and Escapes during the American Civil War* (New York: Charles Scribner's Sons, 1896), 180.

23. Massey, *Ersatz*, 74.

24. Ramsdell, *Behind the Lines*, 84.

25. Lerner, "Money, Prices, and Wages," 27; A. Sellew Roberts, "High Prices and the Blockade in the Confederacy," *South Atlantic Quarterly* 24 (1925), 157.

26. Roberts, "High Prices," 158.

27. John C. Schwab, "Prices in the Confederate States, 1861–65," *Political Science Quarterly* (June 1899): 281–304; idem, *The Confederate States of America* (New York: Charles Scribner's Sons, 1901).

28. Lerner, "Money, Prices, and Wages."

29. Randall and Donald, *The Civil War*, 519.

30. Massey, *Ersatz*, 72.

31. Thomas Senior Berry, *Richmond Commodity Prices, 1861–1865* (Richmond, VA: University of Richmond, Bostwick Press, 1988), 24.

32. Schwab, *The Confederate States*, 177.

33. Schwab, "Prices in the Confederate States," 300; William Diamond, "Imports of the Confederate Government from Europe and Mexico," *Journal of Southern History* (November 1940): 470–503.

34. Roberts, "High Prices," 158.

35. Berry, *Richmond Commodity Prices*, 24.

36. See Stanley Lebergott, "Why the South Lost: Commercial Purposes in the Confederacy, 1861–1865," *Journal of American History* 70 (June 1983): 58–74.

37. Wise, *Lifeline*, 27.

38. Ibid., 26.

39. Confederate States of America, *An Act to Prohibit the Importation of Luxuries or of Articles Not Necessary or of Common Use* (New Haven, CT: Confederate Imprints, 1861–1865; Research Publications, 1974), 10–11.

40. Robinson, "Prohibition in the Confederacy," 51–53.

41. Norman Frank, *Pharmaceutical Conditions and Drug Supply in the Confederacy* (Madison, WI: Institute of the History of Pharmacy, 1955).

42. Joseph T. Durkin, *Confederate Navy Chief: Stephen R. Mallory* (Columbia: University of South Carolina Press, [1954], 1987), 329.

43. Price, "Ships that Tested the Blockade of the Carolina Ports," 232, 236.

44. Confederate States of America, *An Act to Prohibit the Importation of Luxuries*, 10–11.

45. Stanley Lebergott, "Through the Blockade: The Profitability and Extent of Cotton Smuggling, 1861–1865," *Journal of Economic History* 41 (December 1981): 874.

46. Captain (C. Augustus Hobart-Hampden) Roberts, *Never Caught: Personal Adventures Connected with Twelve Successful Trips in Blockade-Running during the American Civil War, 1863–1864* (Wilmington, NC, [1867] 1967), 51.

47. Thomas E. Taylor, *Running the Blockade: A Personal Narrative of Adventures, Risks, and Escapes during the American Civil War* (New York: [Charles Scribner's Sons, 1896] Books for Libraries Press, 1971), 137–38.

48. Roberts, *Never Caught*, 51.

49. Gary Anderson and Robert Tollison, "Political Influence on Civil War Mortality: The Electoral College as a Battlefield," *Defense Economics* 2 (July 1991): 219–33.

50. Eugene H. Roseboom, "Southern Ohio and the Union in 1863," *Mississippi Valley Historical Review* 39 (June 1952): 29–44, esp. 44.

51. Charles W. Ramsdell, "The Confederate Government and the Railroads," *American Historical Review* 22 (July 1917): 794–810.

CHAPTER THREE

INFLATION, NORTH AND SOUTH

In 1865 the Confederate dollar was a mere scrap of paper. But today . . . a Confederate one-dollar bill costs eight dollars U.S. What accounts for "the Confederate miracle"? How can currency backed by a government defunct for over a century be sounder than one backed by the government in Washington? Confederate officials aren't saying, but they seem to have learned a lesson from the severe inflation of 1862–1865. Strict controls on the growth of the Confederate money supply are coupled with a fiscal policy that produces a balanced budget every year.[1]
—John Shelton Reed, *Whistling Dixie: Dispatches from the South* (1990)

BOTH NORTH AND SOUTH resorted to the printing press to finance the war. This chapter will explain the economic rationale of why both governments used inflation and how it impacted on Northern and Southern economies, as well as the role that it played in the outcome of the war. The crucial aspects of this chapter include the following facts:

- Both governments resorted to inflation to finance the war effort and to disguise the true cost of the war
- The Confederate government depended on inflation more than did the Union government
- The Southern economy was more adversely affected by inflation than was the Northern economy,
- Monetary events during the war had a revolutionary impact on money and banking in the United States.

Money is the medium of exchange that serves as the unit in which we do accounting and budgeting. The basis of the terms of loan, salary and wage, and other contracts, money is the means by which we save or store value for future use. Large-scale entrepreneurial projects are only possible because of money and money prices. Without money, the modern exchange economy breaks down into primitive subsistence where life is truly nasty, brutish, and short. Too much money can produce similarly negative results. Increasing the money supply is called monetary inflation, which leads to higher overall prices in the economy or price inflation, and this result reduces the purchasing power of a unit of money such as the dollar. This cause-and-effect relationship is known as the Quantity Theory of Money.

Money that loses value or is "debased" by government can still serve as a medium of exchange, but it no longer functions well as a unit of account, as a standard of deferred payment in long-term contracts, or as a store of value. Inflation therefore undermines the ability of entrepreneurs and bureaucrats to make calculations about the future, of businessmen to form agreements and contracts for production, and of individuals to save and provide the necessary capital for production. When money stops serving as a medium of exchange during a period of hyperinflation, the economy collapses into barter exchange and must reset itself on a different monetary standard.[2]

MONEY AND BANKING BEFORE THE CIVIL WAR

Money and banking were crucial issues that had long divided the country. In the Southern tradition of political economy, the Democratic Party and its historic leaders such as Thomas Jefferson and Andrew Jackson supported "hard money" views. In this tradition, money should consist of gold and silver, banks should not be trusted nor receive any public support, and there should be no national bank.

In much, but not all, of the Northern tradition, the Whig and Republican parties along with their historic leaders such as Alexander Hamilton and Henry Clay supported "easy money" views. In their mercantilist perspective, there is always a shortage of money, so that imports should be discouraged with a high tariff in order to conserve on cash, banks should be encouraged to create credit, and a national bank and currency should be established to increase money and credit as well as to regulate the banking industry and its practices. There were important exceptions to this North-South dichotomy on monetary policy because there were certainly important hard-money advocates in the North and easy-money advocates in the South.

The antebellum economy was one of rapid growth and economic development. The Constitution gave the federal government the power to define money, but its provision was largely a function of the private sector. With some noteworthy exceptions, such as the First and Second Banks of the United States, the federal government was not involved in the banking business and most states only loosely regulated banking, especially between 1837 and the Civil War, a period now known as the Free Banking Era. As we will see, the Civil War dramatically changed money and banking, and these changes have had a lasting impact on American society.

Article 1, Section 8 of the Constitution provides the federal government with the power to "coin money, regulate the Value thereof, and of foreign Coin, and fix the Standard of Weights and Measures." This provision effectively took away the power of individual states to print money and thus created a monetary union in America. A monetary union is an agreement between nations to forgo issuing their own monies and use a common currency much like that now being attempted in Europe with the introduction of the euro. A monetary union removes the obstacles, uncertainties, and other costs associated with the use of multiple currencies. The constitutional monetary union, based on gold and silver, contributed much to America's economic success.

Given this constitutional protection, the ultimate demise of the gold standard required a series of steps in which the country moved from gold coins to paper money by government fiat. These steps occurred in conjunction with the Civil War, World War I, World War II, and the Cold War. The process was finally completed during the Vietnam War, when in 1971 President Richard Nixon closed the "gold window" at which foreign central banks could exchange paper dollars for gold at a fixed rate of one ounce of gold for every $35.

The supply of money prior to the Civil War consisted of gold and silver coins, bank deposits, bank notes, and a small amount of government currency. In 1861 bank notes amounted to more than twelve times government currency. These notes were private currency issued by banks and backed by gold and silver reserves held by the banks and redeemable in a fixed amount of these reserves. The supply of money therefore depended on both the amount of gold and silver and the reserve policy of banks, which independently determined how many notes would be issued against their gold reserves. Money in circulation increased from about $5 per capita in 1800 to approximately $15 per capita in the 1850s.[3] With some important exceptions, the purchasing power of a dollar remained fairly stable over the antebellum period.

One bank note in particular is worth further discussion. The Citizens Bank of Louisiana issued bank notes including a ten-dollar note. This note was very popular because of its widespread acceptability. By state law, the bank backed its note with at least one-third gold reserves while the remaining two-thirds could only be invested by the bank in short-term securities (loans). The high gold reserve requirement and the relative safety of short-term securities made redeeming the notes almost a sure thing and led people to consider the ten-dollar note to be as good as gold. The use of these notes spread throughout the lower South and up the Mississippi and Ohio valleys. Given that the commercial class of New Orleans was French-speaking, the ten-dollar note was printed with *Dix*, the French word for ten, and the English-speaking population called them Dixies. Thus, the famous term for the South was most likely derived from the widespread use of a popular private currency throughout much of the South and West.[4]

Banking in the antebellum period was not a matter of federal regulation or control.[5] State governments had regulatory authority over banks, and potential bankers had to obtain a charter from the state legislature and comply with all the rules and requirements. States often used this regulatory power as a means to obtain revenues and to generate subsidies for their pet pork-barrel projects.[6] However, between 1836 and 1860 more than half the states passed free banking laws, which permitted individuals to start banks that could accept deposits and issue notes without obtaining a special charter from the state legislature. Free banking states imposed fewer restrictions, requirements, and costs, and despite the lack of regulation and the inherent instability of fractional reserve banking, the notes of free banks were generally quite safe and few depositors lost money. When free banks did collapse, the effects were generally localized and did not affect the entire banking system.

The exceptions in the stability and effectiveness of antebellum banking were the two periods when the First and Second Banks of the United States were established and closed, as well as episodes of wildcat banking and state banks. Wildcat banks would accept deposits and issue bank notes but would only agree to redeem the notes in locations where "not even a wildcat would live." Fortunately, this practice was not widespread because people would generally not accept notes from unfamiliar banks. The problem of fraud via wildcat banking was therefore almost unheard of unless it was aided and promoted by the actions of state governments. Despite an outright ban by a decision of the Supreme Court, some state governments established banks that were indeed problematic. Many of these state banks rapidly increased money and credit only to later collapse, leaving taxpayers with the bill while other government banks exploited customers with monopoly rates.

The best single modern source on antebellum money and banking issues is Jeffrey Hummel's article, "The Jacksonians, Banking, and Economic Theory: A Reinterpretation."[7] He provides a succinct overview of President Jackson's "war" against the Second Bank of the United States and all the interpretations that have been applied to it. The traditional view was that the Second Bank was a nascent central bank that provided an effective check on banking practices. The failure to renew its charter therefore unleashed destructive and uncontrolled banking practices that caused severe economic problems.

The revisionist school, which has come to dominate the debate, found that the Bank War and Jackson's monetary policies did not have much of an effect on banking or the economy. The Free Banking Era that followed the Second Bank essentially created a passive money and banking system, so that the macroeconomic problems of this period were the result of international problems imported into the economy. The revisionists consider the control of banking at the state level to be an improvement over the national control exercised by the Second Bank of the United States.

However, as Hummel makes clear, free banking legislation was really a compromise between the Whigs' preference for an inflationary nationalized banking system and the Jacksonian laissez-faire view that government should play no role at all. Free banking legislation actually placed several conditions on banks that restricted competition and gave them the government's seal of approval to issue paper money not completely backed by gold. The hard-money Jacksonians would have preferred a system where gold and silver coin served as money and banks could not issue paper money that was not completely backed by metal reserves and immediately redeemable in gold or silver.

The debate was once characterized as two-dimensional, with the traditional view blaming all of the monetary problems of the antebellum era on Jackson's destruction of the Second Bank and the revisionist view that state-regulated "free banks" caused no economic problems at all. Hummel's analysis, however, makes clear the multidimensional character of the debate. First, he shows that the revisionists support unsound banking practices such as low levels of bank reserves and disparage gold money because it costs real resources to mine gold and mint it into coins. A logical extension of the revisionist view would be to adopt fiat-paper money, but historically this approach has been highly inflationary. Also, their claim that all macroeconomic problems were international in their source only pushes the question of macroeconomic stability beyond the border, but it does not explain it.

In the direction of hard-money Jacksonians, Hummel also extends the debate to include the "true" laissez-faire view that government should not intervene in banking, that market competition would place the economy on a gold standard, and that competition and the legal process would drive banks to hold reserves equal to 100 percent of the notes or demand deposits that they issue. The efforts of the hard-money advocates in the United States and Britain led to a much-improved system of money and banking, but their failure to completely achieve their policy goals left the economy susceptible to the fluctuations of the business cycle and bank panics.

Naturally, this debate has been subjected to statistical test-ing, and the results clearly suggest that Jackson's reforms were an improvement but were not perfect. The evidence shows that commercial banking in the antebellum period was conservative and that wildcat practices were of little consequence. The gen-eral public became conservative with their money and was more sensitive to the opportunity cost of holding money after the down-fall of the Second Bank, so that as interest rates rose, people held less cash and put more money in the bank to earn those higher rates of interest. The general public also tended to hold a larger overall level of specie relative to money deposited in banks, indi-cating a more cautious attitude on their part. Banks also acted more conservatively in the sense that they considered their gold holdings as the necessary reserves to be retained against poten-tial withdrawals rather than as excess reserves available to make new loans if interest rates increased.

The higher level of specie reserves also meant that the bank-ing system's ability to expand the money supply in the form of bank notes and demand deposits was cut nearly in half, so that internal and international shocks would have a much less severe impact on the economy and produce milder business cycles. The general public was much more conservative and banks were more stable. This evidence clearly refutes the traditional view that the destruction of the Second Bank ushered in an era of irresponsible wildcat banking. It also undermines the revisionist view that the Bank War had no effect because it did indeed change the behav-ior of bankers and the public. Marie Sushka, who conducted the statistical analysis of this period, concluded that the Panic of 1837 was probably the result of the economy adapting to the condi-tions of a more stable monetary system.[8] In any case, it did help set the stage for the most significant two-decade economic ex-pansion in American, if not world, history.

INFLATION AND PUBLIC FINANCE

War is an enormous burden on the economy. Labor and capi-tal must be diverted from productive to military purposes. Labor is reallocated to fighting the war, and the ensuing deaths and in-juries further reduce current and future production. Labor is also reallocated away from the production of civilian goods to the production of military goods, such as guns, ammunition, and fortifications. Capital is diverted from the production of civilian goods to military goods, such as from plows to cannons; and capital goods are also diverted from civilian use to the military, as in the case of the railroads.

Governments can resort to taxation, borrowing, inflation, confiscation, and conscription in order to finance a war. Most governments resort to a combination of these methods, but the mix of financing methods is a crucial choice because each one has different effects on the economy. Given that all the effects are negative, a poor public finance choice in terms of both the method and size of revenue could have severe consequences on the economy and thus on the ability to wage war.

Despite all of its flaws, taxation can be the best method of public finance because the burden is relatively well-known and certain. If the rates are held to the lowest possible level and placed on the largest possible base, tax policy would be credible in the sense that taxpayers view the rates as equitable and not subject to future increases. This form of public finance should have the least negative impact on the economy and the least amount of distortion between industries. Taxation also constrains the government's ability to extract resources from the economy because high taxation will reduce taxpayers' compliance and increase opposition to the government and its war effort. Open and honest public finance improves a government's credibility with potential creditors.

Borrowing is also a good method of financing war under the right conditions. If you can borrow the money from foreigners and spend the money on foreign products, then you do not drain resources from your economy and borrowing can effectively spread the cost of the war into the postwar period. Many governments, however, cannot borrow the funds because foreigners doubt their chances of winning the war or their ability to pay off the debt after a victory. The result is that governments that are expected to win easy victories can borrow money on good terms, but those with dubious prospects will only be able to sell unsecured debt at deep discounts and high interest rates. Therefore, borrowing is only a good economic option when it is largely unnecessary.

Conscription and confiscation are methods by which governments compel labor and capital into the war effort. These policies usually give labor and capital owners some compensation, but the difference between government compensation and market price is critical. If the government gives compensation near true market values, then resources owners will not be significantly harmed and production will not be highly distorted or discouraged. Proper compensation will not engender opposition to the war effort, nor will it encourage the government to acquire and waste resources, but it also will not provide many additional resources because the compensation will have to come from some other source. If the government offers little compensation to conscripts and capital owners, opposition to the war effort will tend to increase, private sector production will be greatly discouraged, and governments will tend to acquire and waste too many resources and thus hurt the economy and war effort further.

Inflation, or the creation of new money to finance war, is by far the easiest form of public finance for the government, but it is also the most damaging to the economy. Printing new money only requires a little paper and ink and does not produce the negative political ramifications that result from taxation and confiscation. In fact, when the government spends its paper money, citizens happily view the regime as a new customer for their products and labor. Typically, citizens will tend to blame the effect of this inflation and higher prices not on the government but on speculators, middlemen, and foreigners.

Inflation has two important disadvantages over other means of financing war. First, inflation distorts prices, wages, and capital values and thus undermines the ability of producers and consumers to make rational economic decisions. This distortion greatly hampers an economy's ability to allocate resources efficiently and therefore reduces its ability to produce civilian and military goods. Second, because inflation is such a relatively easy method of acquiring resources and goods, governments naturally have the tendency to drain too many resources from the economy and to waste too much of those resources.

Given the high economic costs of inflationary finance, it would be advantageous to rely on taxation to finance war. For example, in his analysis of Austria during World War I, Joseph Schumpeter concluded, "it is clear that strictly speaking we could have squeezed the necessary money out of the private economy just as the goods were squeezed out of it. This could have been done by taxes which would have looked stifling, but which would in fact have been no more oppressive than the devaluation of money which was their alternative."[9] Schumpeter notes that the reason for inflationary war finance is not necessity, but politics. Joseph Salerno explained that financing war via inflation is employed by politicians to conceal the cost of war "beneath the veil of inflation." Inflation therefore not only obscures people's ability to make rational economic decisions, but it also impedes the ability to calculate the true cost of government activities, such as war.[10]

INFLATION IN THE NORTH

The classic study of Union inflation was Wesley Clair Mitchell's century-old *History of the Greenbacks*.[11] Initially the war was to be financed with the use of government bonds, tax revenues would be used to pay the normal expenditures of government, and the gold standard would be retained. However, this system quickly collapsed in late 1861 and the first of three legal tender acts was passed in February 1862 with a total of $450 million in greenbacks authorized for issue. When an economy has two types of money, such as gold and paper, and they are both defined in the same units, such as dollars, Gresham's Law states that bad money will drive good money out of circulation. And in accordance with Gresham's Law, greenback dollars quickly displaced gold dollars as the circulating medium of exchange.

The value of greenbacks quickly depreciated in terms of gold and fell to a low point of only 35 cents worth of gold on July 11, 1864. Amazingly, the Union currency had depreciated as much in three short years as the dollar has in the thirty years since the United States went off the gold standard. The prices of goods appreciated in terms of greenbacks from an index value of 100 in 1860 to a maximum of 216.8 in 1865. Citizens tended to blame higher prices on business, speculators, and foreigners. Some government officials believed that speculators in the gold market were somehow causing the value of greenbacks to fall, but the real culprit for inflation was the government itself.

In addition to an ever-increasing supply of greenbacks, Mitchell showed that the value of greenbacks in terms of gold would change on the basis of expectations that in turn were based on peoples' estimated probability that the greenbacks would be redeemed for gold after the war. Battlefield losses were associated with declines in value while victories meant higher values for the greenback.

Higher prices also meant that the Union government would have to issue more greenbacks in order to purchase war supplies and pay its soldiers. Because the Union government would eventually have to pay its war debts and redeem the greenbacks in gold, Mitchell investigated whether the use of greenbacks increased or decreased the cost of the war. He calculated that the greenbacks had increased the real cost of the war to the government itself by $528 million. Of course, the politicians who borrowed and spent the money during the war were not necessarily the same ones who had to pay off the debt and redeem the greenbacks after the war.

Mitchell also found that the switch from gold to paper had important and potent secondary effects. These included an illusory increase in property values, an increase in extravagance and the purchase of luxury goods, a crippling of economic efficiency, and a decrease in real wages for farmers, laborers, professionals, teachers, and soldiers.[12] As expected, the Union's inflationary finances created an illusion of general prosperity that greatly upset the ability of entrepreneurs, workers, consumers, and bureaucrats to make accurate economic calculations.[13]

In recent years, Mitchell's analysis has been confirmed with advanced statistical techniques, and this body of evidence supports Salerno's view that inflation is used to hide the cost of war and that inflation has highly deleterious effects on the economy. Economists such as Charles Calomiris continue to study the market for greenbacks in order to better understand the history of the Civil War and its aftermath, measuring the impact of real world events by looking at changes in prices and currency values.[14] This evidence also is useful in answering an important ongoing

debate in economic theory as to whether price inflation and deflation are caused by monetary or real factors. Monetarist economists tend to believe that inflation is purely a monetary
phenomenon and they assemble evidence in an attempt to defend the Quantity Theory of Money. Keynesian economists tend
to believe that inflation is the result of real factors and they present
evidence that real factors determine the price level.[15] Both approaches offer important insights into the phenomena of inflation, and the real truth probably lies somewhere in between. The
Austrian School, for example, claims that the quantity of money
and real factors are both important but that the value or purchasing power of money is based on the subjective valuations of individuals, just like the price of goods. The Austrians therefore regard
both the Monetarists' quantity-only approach and the Keynesians'
real-only approach as incomplete for understanding the value of
money. The evidence presented by Mitchell and many others
seems to support this view.

For example, economists have applied new statistical techniques to study the day-to-day value of greenbacks in terms of
gold to determine the statistically significant events of the war
(see Table 3-1). They found seven significant dates where a "structural break" in the data occurred and was followed by a period
of significant price movement in the same direction as the original break. Two such "breaks" corresponded with well-known historical events, Antietam and the Emancipation Proclamation
(October 23, 1862) and the Gettysburg and Vicksburg victories
(July 6, 1863), but they also found important dates that historians
have neglected, such as the decision to issue $300 million more
greenbacks (January 8, 1863), Jubal Early's raid on Washington
(July 12, 1864), Finance Committee Chairman William Pitt
Fessenden's meeting with New York bankers, and Abraham
Lincoln's rumored pursuit of peace (August 24, 1864). They even
found two dates that remain a mystery: August 27, 1863, which
might have reflected early uncertainties concerning the presidential contest of 1864; and March 8, 1865, which might have been
associated with the fall of the port city of Wilmington, North
Carolina, and the coming collapse of the Confederate army.[16] Their
findings clearly show that the value of money and prices can
change on the basis of people's subjective evaluations, informa-

tion, events, and even nonevents. Thus, the quantity-only and real-only approaches tell only part of the story, and a more holistic approach is required to understand inflation.

Table 3-1. Major Statistical Events in the Greenback Market

Date	Percentage Change	Long-run Percentage Change	Major Event
10/23/62	-0.44	-8.8	Antietam, Emancipation Proclamation
1/8/63	-1.40	-28.0	$300 million in greenbacks
7/6/63	1.56	31.2	Gettysburg, Vicksburg
8/27/63	-0.63	-12.6	???
7/12/64	4.80	96.0	Early retreats, Fessenden confers with New York bankers
8/24/64	0.40	8.0	Peace rumors
3/8/65	2.60	52.0	Fall of Wilmington?

Source: Kristen L. Willard, Timothy W. Guinnane, and Harvey S. Rosen, "Turning Points in the Civil War: Views from the Greenback Market," *American Economic Review* 86, no. 4 (September 1996): 1009. Reprinted by permission of the American Economic Association.

Table 3-2: Northern Prices and Real Wage Rates, 1860–1865
(Base Year 1860 = 100)

Year	Prices (dollars)	Real Wages (percentage)
1860	100	100
1861	101	100
1862	113	93
1863	139	84
1864	176	77
1865	175	82

Source: Jeremy Atack and Peter Passell, *A New Economic View of American History from Colonial Times to 1940*, 2d ed. (New York: W. W. Norton, 1994), 367, Table 13.5. © 1994 by Jeremy Atack and Peter Passell. © 1979 by Susan Lee and Peter Passell. Reprinted by permission of W. W. Norton.

Economists have investigated and confirmed Mitchell's finding of lower real wage rates. Even though nominal wages were rising, the evidence presented in Table 3-2 shows that rising prices meant that the real purchasing power of those wages was declining. Economists have also been concerned with what caused these lagging wage rates.[17] Were lower real wages the result of "real" changes in the economy, such as disruptions in trade caused by the war, or were they the result of monetary factors that prevented wage rate increases from keeping up with the prices of goods and services? Stephen DeCanio and Joel Mokyr estimated that one-third of the wage lag was due to real factors and two-thirds were due to monetary factors. This estimate would also support the case for a more holistic approach to understanding inflation and the value of money. Inflation caused real wages to fall, and only with the end of the war and a rising greenback did real wages begin to recover.[18]

INFLATION IN THE SOUTH

Eugene Lerner conducted the classic study of the monetary history of the Confederacy. He constructed an index of the total stock of money in the Confederacy and an index of wholesale prices based on prices in four Southern cities. This information was then used to describe price movements in various parts of the South and the impact of the blockade on the Southern economy. Lerner also examined the impact of inflation on the real purchasing power of wage rates in the South, and his results confirm several important theoretical insights concerning monetary inflation during the Civil War.

In January 1861 the total stock of money, including bank notes and bank deposits, in the Southern states amounted to $94.6 million. The total amount of bank notes and bank deposits would grow to over $268 million by January 1864. In June 1861 the Confederate government had placed only $1.1 million of its notes into circulation, but that figure increased to $826.8 million by January 1864. Therefore, the total stock of money increased from $94.6 million to $1,094.9 million over this three-year period. In Table 3-3 the money stock is indexed and shows that the money stock increased by 1,057 percent, with the index level increasing from 100 to 1,160.

Based on the Quantity Theory of Money we would expect this increase in the stock of money to cause higher prices and reduced purchasing power of the Confederate dollar because governments, businesses, and individuals had more money to purchase the goods and services available in the marketplace. Lerner attempted to calculate the effect of this increase in the stock of money on prices by calculating a price index of wholesale commodities in four Southern cities. The results of his calculations show that prices increased by 92 times their prewar level. Figure 3-1 shows Lerner's index of the Southern money supply as well as his index of prices in the Confederacy. Money supply and prices seem to run parallel until the Battle of Gettysburg and the fall of Vicksburg, when prices began to rise rapidly while the money supply grew at a slow rate. As the Confederacy shrunk in size due to military defeat, Confederate paper money would concentrate in the remaining area and drive up prices even higher.

Table 3-3. Lerner's Index of the Southern Money Supply, 1861–1864 (Base January 1861 = 100)

Date	Money Supply Index
January 1861	100
April 1861	130
June 1861	130
October 1861	180
January 1862	250
April 1862	300
June 1862	330
October 1862	500
January 1863	690
April 1863	870
June 1863	960
October 1863	1,130
January 1864	1,160

Source: Eugene M. Lerner, "Money, Prices, and Wages in the Confederacy, 1861–1865," *Journal of Political Economy* 62 (February 1955): 20–40. Reprinted by permission of the University of Chicago Press.

Thus, prices increased much more than the supply of money, so that in January 1865, $100 had the same purchasing power of only one dollar in January 1861. Two additional factors account for this discrepancy. First, real factors in the economy changed as production plummeted due to the diversion of resources and the destruction caused by the war, the disruptions of the naval blockade, and the problems of economic calculation caused by massive monetary inflation. Second, subjective evaluations of Confederate money caused changes in its value in response to military victories and defeats and led to a general panic among holders of Confederate dollars as defeat became apparent.

Figure 3.1. Indices of the Money and Price Level
in the Confederacy, 1861–1865 (January 1861 = 100)

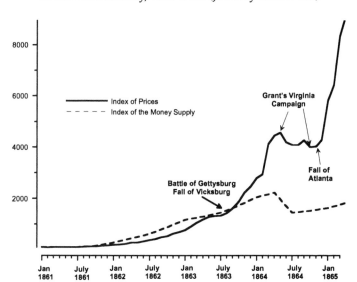

Sources: Roger L. Ransom, "Economics of the Civil War," EH.Net Encyclopedia, ed. Robert Whaples, August 25, 2001, http://www.eh.net/encyclopedia/contents/ransom.civil.war.us.php. Based on Roger L. Ransom, "The Historical Statistics of the Confederacy," in *The Historical Statistics of the United States, Millennial Edition*, ed. Susan Carter and Richard Sutch (New York: Cambridge University Press, 2002). Reprinted by permission of EH.Net and Roger L. Ransom.

The Confederate government raised the bulk of its resources from the printing press, the easiest means at its disposal. The Union government took a more balanced approach and raised nearly two-thirds of its revenues from loans and a balanced combination of taxes and inflation for the remainder. Because inflation is such an easy means of finance, it encouraged the Confederate administration to extract and waste large volumes of resources. The small amount of loans available to the Confederate government deprived it of the least destructive form of finance and one that enlists the support of one's creditors, particularly foreign creditors. In Table 3-4, a comparison of Confederate finance is made to that of the Union government, the Revolutionary War, and the War of 1812. The Confederacy used the greatest percentage of inflation and the smallest percentage of loans.

Table 3-4. Comparison of War Finance

	Confederate	Union	1776	1812
Loans	21.3%	64.5%	29.5%	49.0%
Taxes	10.5%	16.5%	8.8%	28.5%
Currency	61.7%	16.5%	57.4%	16.3%
Other	6.5%	2.5%	4.3%	6.2%

Source: John Munro Godfrey, *Monetary Expansion in the Confederacy* (New York: Arno Press, 1978), 14. Reprinted by permission of John Munro Godfrey.

Inflation had tremendous adverse consequences on the Southern economy and citizens' morale. People blamed the huge increases in prices on speculators and blockade-runners and accused others of being unpatriotic. Higher prices meant lower real incomes. They also had an adverse effect on the ability of people to make long-term economic plans and stymied the efforts of entrepreneurs to make accurate calculations regarding the investment of capital and output decision.[19] Table 3-5 shows the annual price index for the Confederacy and the corresponding real wage rate. The real wage index shows the intense poverty that people experienced in the Civil War South because real earning power fell to only 11 percent of its prewar level.

Table 3-5. Southern Prices and Real Wage Rates, 1860–1865 (Base Year 1860 = 100)

Year	Prices (dollars)	Real Wages (percentage)
1860	100	100
1861	121	86
1862	388	35
1863	1,452	19
1864	3,992	11

Source: Eugene M. Lerner, "Money, Prices, and Wages in the Confederacy, 1861–1865" (Ph.D. diss., University of Chicago, 1954).

While everyone criticizes Confederate inflation, many critics argue that the Confederates did not inflate enough or that the method brought in insufficient resources. What, they ask, is the alternative? The best alternative from the economic point of view is non-inflationary finance, based on taxation and borrowing, and possibly the sale of assets. The beauty of noninflationary finance is that it protects the local economy, enlists the support of creditors, and signals them that their investments are safe and their money is spent efficiently. Noninflationary finance, in reducing the amount of resources available to the Confederate government, would have forced its officials to rely on a more decentralized and defensive military strategy. It might also have made them more cooperative with their state governments, the business community, the slave population, and foreign nations and forced them to make the tough decisions they were unwilling to face under inflationary finance until the final days of the war.

THE MONETARY LEGACY OF THE CIVIL WAR

The Civil War caused a sea change in the institutions of money and banking. Before the war the monetary system was essentially a private system with gold and silver coins circulating as the medium of exchange. The vast bulk of money consisted of privately issued bank notes, with most banks maintaining high capital and reserve ratios to maintain the acceptability of their notes.

After the war, money was dominated by government greenbacks, and the free coinage of silver was ended in 1873. While the redemption of greenbacks for gold is generally viewed as necessary and positive, the process of redemption was less than perfect and had some negative economic effects. While there were certainly some minor monetary problems prior to the war, monetary problems after the war led to the formation of large scale political movements such as Free Silver, the Greenback Party, and the presidential campaigns of William Jennings Bryant. Their primary goal was to fight the persistent artificial storage of money that resulted after the war due to federal control of money and banking but not, as their critics have often alleged, to put the country on an inflationary binge.[20]

Banking was also fundamentally changed as a result of the war. Prior to the conflict the federal government had little impact on banking. States had the authority to charter and regulate banks, but several states adopted free banking legislation, which greatly reduced barriers to entry and exit and imposed few costs and constraints. As a result, banking was highly competitive and served its various roles in the economy well. Problems such as wildcat banking and bank failures are now known to have been relatively rare and to have imposed few costs on customers or on the economy at large.

The National Banking Act changed all that. By taxing the notes of state banks it drove the industry to obtain new national charters and thus to fall into a nationalized system of bank regulations and controls. With a national currency and a national banking system, money and banking, which are central to the healthy functioning of the economy, were now more uniform and under the control of the central government, but they were also more likely to become subject to problems of contagion, such as panics. For example, in a free banking system, if a bank were to suffer from bad loans, its depositors might withdraw their money (bank run) and transfer it to other banks, making the surviving banks stronger. In a national banking environment, the problems in one bank would lead to a bank run but could also have a contagious effect on other banks and cause a bank panic across the economy.[21]

There were panics before the war, but they tended to be caused by real factors, such as war, or exogenous factors, such as money and credit conditions in Europe. Pre-Civil War panics tended to be shortlived and to exhibit most of their effects in commercial banking centers. After the war, panics occurred more often, were more domestic in nature, and had more severe and widespread effects.

The book by Frank Baum, *The Wonderful Wizard of Oz*, and the popular movie that was based on it, was an allegory to the growing monetary problems and political populism of the late nineteenth century. The Emerald (green) City is Washington and the Wizard of Oz (ounce of gold) is the president, who manipulates the population on behalf of the big-city banks. The Tin Man, Scarecrow, and Munchkins represent different groups of people while the Cowardly Lion represents William Jennings Bryant and Dorothy stands for "everyman," the average, good-natured citizen, who does not have a clue about the underlying causes of the problems of society. The Yellow Brick Road is the gold standard. The silver (in the book) slippers were the magic cure to get Dorothy home, just as the Free Silver movement and the free coinage of silver were the magic cure for all sorts of social problems because it would create a more fluid and flexible monetary system and take power away from the big-city banks of the East.[22] Baum's story parallels the American banking system where the government and big banks controlled the economy in support of the industrial and financial interests in the East to the detriment of farmers, labor, and rural America, especially in the South and West. The notion that the new national banking system that replaced the largely laissez-faire system was somehow in the public interest is hard to defend. Three leading mainstream monetary economists studied the national system and found that if they assumed the system was based on public interest motives to improve the economy and help everyone in society, then the system was a colossal failure:

> The provision of the Acts of 1863 and 1865 that established the national banking system were designed to remedy two perceived defects of the antebellum state banking system. One was the circulation of a wide variety of state bank notes, often at a discount, which made for an inefficient payments system. The second defect was instability of the note issue, marked by over issue, bank runs and failures, and periodic suspensions of convertibility into specie. To remedy the first defect, national bank issues of U.S. bond-secured currency replaced state bank notes. To remedy the second defect, stringent reserve and capital requirements, oversight, and regulation by the Comptroller of the Currency were conditions for national bank charters. Unfortunately, the remedies did not work as intended by the architects of the national banking system. Instead, the system was characterized by monetary and cyclical instability, four banking panics, frequent stock market crashes, and other financial disturbances."[23]

It is therefore more accurate to describe the national banking system as a major political victory for the Hamiltonian and Whig tradition that sought government control of money and banking and the promotion of government debt and easy credit policies.

We have seen that both Union and Confederate governments resorted to the printing press to finance their war efforts. The Confederate government, however, used inflation to provide a significantly larger proportion of its revenues. While this policy certainly helped to disguise the cost of the war, it also had a devastating effect on the Southern economy and encouraged the government in Richmond to absorb and waste too many economic

resources in the war effort. In addition to being a contributing
cause for the Confederate defeat and the Union victory, the war
also had a revolutionary impact on the money and banking institutions of America and can be described as an important victory
of the Hamiltonian tradition of "capitalism."

NOTES

1. John Shelton Reed, *Whistling Dixie: Dispatches from the South* (Columbia: University of Missouri Press, 1990), 5, 8.
2. For more on the theory of money and inflation see Ludwig von
Mises, *The Theory of Money and Credit*, http://www.econlib.org/library/
Mises/msTtoc.html.
3. Charles A. Conant, *A History of Modern Banks of Issue* (New York:
Augustus M. Kelley, [1896] 1969), 395.
4. Howard L. Sacks and Judith Rose Sacks, *Way Up North in Dixie: A
Black Family's Claim to the Confederate Anthem* (Washington, DC:
Smithsonian Institution Press, 1993).
5. Richard Sylla, "Forgotten Men of Money: Private Bankers in Early
U.S. History," *Journal of Economic History* 36 (March 1976): 173–88.
6. Richard Sylla, John B. Legler, and John J. Wallis, "Banks and State
Public Finance in the New Republic: The United States, 1790–1860," *Journal of Economic History* 47 (June 1987): 391–403.
7. Jeffrey Rogers Hummel, "The Jacksonians, Banking, and Economic
Theory: A Reinterpretation," *Journal of Libertarian Studies* 2 (Summer
1978): 151–65.
8. Marie Elizabeth Sushka, "The Antebellum Money Market and the
Economic Impact of the Bank War," *Journal of Economic History* 36 (December 1976): 809–35.
9. Joseph Schumpeter, "The Crisis of the Tax State," in *The Economics and Sociology of Capitalism*, ed. Richard Swedberg (Princeton, NJ:
Princeton University Press, 1991), 121.
10. Joseph Salerno, "War and the Money Machine: Concealing the
Costs of War beneath the Veil of Inflation," in *The Costs of War: America's
Pyrrhic Victories*, ed. John V. Denson (New Brunswick, NJ: Transaction
Publishers, 1997), 367–87.
11. Wesley Clair Mitchell, *A History of the Greenbacks, with Special
Reference to the Economic Consequences of Their Issue: 1862–65* (Chicago:
University of Chicago Press, 1903); idem, *Gold, Prices, and Wages under
the Greenback Standard* (Berkeley: University of California Press, 1908).
12. Wesley C. Mitchell, "Greenbacks and the Cost of the Civil War,"
Journal of Political Economy 5 (March 1897): 117–56.
13. Amos W. Stetson, *Is Our Prosperity a Delusion? Our National Debt
and Currency* (Boston: A. Williams, 1864); Eugene M. Lerner, "Investment Uncertainty during the Civil War—A Note on the McCormick
Brothers," *Journal of Economic History* 16 (March 1956): 34–40.

14. Charles W. Calomiris, "Price and Exchange Rate Determination during the Greenback Suspension," *Oxford Economic Papers* 40 (December 1988): 719–50; idem, "Greenback Resumption and Silver Risk: The Economics and Politics of Monetary Regime Change in the United States, 1862–1900," Working Paper 4166, Cambridge, MA: National Bureau of Economic Research, 1992.

15. Milton Friedman, "Price, Income, and Monetary Changes in Three Wartime Periods," *American Economic Review* 42 (May 1952): 612–43; Michael D. Bordo and Anna J. Schwartz, "Money and Prices in the Nineteenth Century: An Old Debate Rejoined," *Journal of Economic History* 40 (March 1980): 61–67.

16. Kristen L. Willard, Timothy W. Guinnane, and Harvey S. Rosen, "Turning Points in the Civil War: Views from the Greenback Market," Working Paper 5381, Cambridge MA: National Bureau of Economic Research, December 1995.

17. Rubin A. Kessel and Arman A. Alchien, "Real Wage Rates in the North during the Civil War: Mitchell's Data Reinterpreted," *Journal of Law and Economics* 2 (1959): 95–113.

18. Stephen J. DeCanio and Joel Mokyr, "Inflation and the Wage Law during the American Civil War," *Explorations in Economic History* 14 (October 1977): 311–36.

19. Edwin B. Coddington, "The Activities and Attitudes of a Confederate Business Man: Gazaway B. Lamar," *Journal of Southern History* 9 (February 1943): 3–36.

20. Marshall Gramm and Phil Gramm, "The Free Silver Movement in America: A Reinterpretation," presented in New Orleans, Louisiana, at the Southern Economic Association, November 2002.

21. Robert B. Ekelund Jr., Charles D. DeLorme, and Mark Thornton, "The Money-Creation Model: An Alternative Pedagogy," *Journal of Economic Education* 22 (Fall 1991): 317–24.

22. Henry M. Littlefield, "The Wizard of Oz: Parable on Populism," *American Quarterly* 16 (Spring 1964): 47–58; Hugh Rockoff, "The 'Wizard of Oz' as a Monetary Allegory," *Journal of Political Economy* 98 (August 1990): 739–60.

23. Michael D. Bordo, Peter Rappoport, and Anna J. Schwartz, "Money versus Credit Rationing: Evidence for the National Banking Era, 1880–1914," in *Strategic Factors in Nineteenth-Century American Economic Growth*, ed. Claudia Goldin and Hugh Rockoff (Chicago: University of Chicago Press, 1992), 189–23.

CHAPTER FOUR

CONSEQUENCES OF THE WAR

Every unprejudiced person can naturally have no
doubt that war can really cause no economic boom
. . . war prosperity is like the prosperity that an earthquake or a plague brings. The earthquake means good
business for construction workers, and cholera improves the business of physicians, pharmacists, and
undertakers; but no one has for that reason yet sought
to celebrate earthquakes and cholera as stimulators of
the productive forces in the general interest.[1]
—Ludwig von Mises, *Nation, State, and Economy* (1983)

MUCH HAS BEEN written about Reconstruction and the postwar
economy, but rarely from the perspective of economic theory. In
this chapter we examine the central issues of the impact of the
war on the postwar economy and on the black population of the
South, changes in economic institutions, such as banking and technology, and the long-term legacy of the war. Economic theory is
employed here to critique the scholarly research on these sub-
jects and to develop a clear and consistent portrait of the consequences of the war.

Historians have generally treated the economic impact of the
Civil War in a positive fashion. In addition to the emancipation
of slaves, the war established the United States as a global power,
and Republican economic policy laid the foundation for an industrial revolution in America, the rise of big business, and the
role of the United States as an economic leader in the world. We
show that the war itself had little to do with the positive developments in the postwar economy and that its actual impact was
to retard economic growth and to cause important distortions that
harmed both black and white rural populations and led to important reform movements such as Populism. Although statistical
evidence has made economic historians increasingly suspect about

the benefits of the war, economic theory provides the guidelines for ascertaining its impact even in the absence of such statistics.

THE ECONOMIC IMPACT OF THE CIVIL WAR

The well-known results of the Civil War include the maintenance of the Union (with West Virginia seceding from Virginia), over one million people killed or wounded, the abolition of black slavery, and three new amendments to the Constitution. Historians have generally given a positive spin to the economic effects of the war and hailed the accomplishments made in its aftermath, such as the intercontinental railroad, technological improvements, and the development of large-scale heavy industry. This perspective, however, ignores one of the most basic lessons of economics: that war is destructive, not constructive. The famous French economist Frédéric Bastiat made this lesson clear in his parable of the broken window. A young hoodlum throws a brick that smashes the storefront window of a baker. The crowd that gathers speculates that the incident will create work for the glazier who fixes the window and who in turn will have more money to spend on his family, which in turn will stimulate even more spending and employment.[2]

The crowd, however, is mistaken. They have forgotten that the money paid by the baker to the glazier would have been spent by the baker on goods for his family or invested in his business, thus creating a similar stream of spending and employment. The only difference is that the baker and society are worse off due to the broken window. If the crowd had been correct, prosperity could be assured for all of us if only there were enough hoodlums willing to smash our windows on a regular basis.

We should not be too hard on the crowd because professional economists themselves are often guilty of the same mistake. It is a common misconception that certain wars have produced economic benefits, with the classic example being that the massive industrial output required by World War II brought an end to the Great Depression.[3] It is also common to find economic analysts touting the benefits of hurricanes, earthquakes, and other natural disasters in the wake of the destruction because it will stimulate reconstruction and homebuilding.[4] As Bastiat warns, the economic benefits of war and natural disasters are "seen" while the economic costs are "unseen" and of necessity are larger than the alleged benefits. It is indeed an ill wind that does not blow some good, but it is ghoulish and professionally irresponsible for economic analysts to extol the benefits of such disasters and wars. Another possible example of the benefits of war is post-World War II Germany and Japan. Both countries experienced high rates of economic growth during the postwar period, which is often explained by the fact that the devastation of the war allowed Germany and Japan to rebuild using the latest technological advances, which were financed by American foreign aid. However, Mancur Olson found that the growth of the German and Japanese economies was largely attributable to the fact that the war destroyed economic institutions of these two countries, such as price controls, unions, regulations, and fascist bureaucracies. It was in this bureaucratic vacuum that entrepreneurship and capital accumulation were allowed to thrive, not in the wartime destruction of physical capital and labor. It is important to note that even this benefit of war is only in terms of higher growth rates, not in the absolute standard of living, and this type of economic vitality could be achieved less destructively through legislation.[5]

Economic theory, then, would suggest that the American Civil War was a destructive rather than constructive event. It is obvious that the war reduced the supply of labor and that a vast amount of capital was destroyed or greatly depreciated during the war. It is also known that farmland went fallow, railroads and shipping assets were reduced, financial and commercial ties were severed, and technological, educational, scientific, and cultural opportunities were lost. This chapter will investigate this destruction. In addition, the aftereffects of war will be examined to determine if the conflict had any possible benefits for the postwar economy. Special notice will be made not only of institutional changes, such as those analyzed by Olson, but also of the most notable institutional change resulting from the war: the emancipation of slave labor.

THE POSTWAR ECONOMY

Historical understanding of the postwar period tends to downplay the direct effects of the war and to jump into the political problems of Reconstruction. To the extent that the postwar economy is discussed, we find that at this time the power of industrial capitalism has been released from the clutches of agrarianism and the slave power. The postwar period is treated as the nation's industrial revolution, the rise of the big corporations, the completion of America's so-called Manifest Destiny, and, oddly, an era of laissez-faire economic policy. Interestingly, while historians of the Civil War have tended to emphasize its positive economic impacts, historians in general have not made an uncritical assessment of the postwar period. For example, the period of industrial revolution is also considered one of capitalistic exploitation, with the leaders of the giant corporations dubbed "evil robber barons." As a result, Populism and Unionism are portrayed as a political movement that rises up to defend the individual against organized business interests.

With the help of economic theory, we can show that the divergent and seemingly contradictory views of the Civil War and the postwar economy are all part of the same consistent history. The direct effects of the war were negative, and they did have a negative impact on the postwar economy. Many of these results can now be discerned from the statistical evidence provided by the new economic historians.

The war certainly did release industrialism and corporatism and complete our Manifest Destiny, and thus led to uneven economic gains and the rise of Populism. The Republican economic agenda was designed to achieve those results at the expense of unorganized interests such as small business, farming, and labor. These groups benefited the least from the postwar recovery, and they formed the backbone of the Populist movement. Understanding the interest groups supporting the Republican Party also provides some understanding of the economic fate of the freed slaves in the postwar economy.

WAS THE WAR A BOON TO THE ECONOMY?

Historians have tended to treat the Civil War as a boon to industry and the American economy. Thomas C. Cochran cites several prominent historians such as Charles and Mary Beard, Arthur Schlesinger Sr., Harold Faulkner, Richard Hofstadter, William Miller, Daniel Aaron, Gilbert Fite, Jim Reese, and Denis Brogan, who variously praised the impact of the conflict on wartime production and its stimulating effect on postwar economic and industrial development. Cochran then attacked the notion that the Civil War was beneficial to the economy. He examined statistical data on industrial production and found that, in general, there was not a strong case for a positive impact and that the war had a retarding effect on industry and the economy. For example, he showed that pig iron production grew substantially before and after the war but managed only a 1 percent increase during the conflict. Cochran also found little support for the claims of beneficial effects of the Civil War on postwar development. He concludes with this speculation: "From most standpoints the Civil War was a national disaster, but Americans like to see their history in terms of optimism and progress. Perhaps the war was put in a perspective suited to the culture by seeing it as good because in addition to achieving freedom for the Negro it brought about industrial progress."[6]

The Beards' claim that the Civil War was a spur to industry and the rise of the American economy is based on the laissez-faire philosophy of the Republican Party and its success in implementing its major policy goals, such as subsidies to the intercontinental railroads, the establishment of a national currency, and the protective tariff. Stephen Salsbury defended the Beards against Cochran's evidence by arguing that several measures of industrial output increased after the war. He challenged Cochran by claiming that the ingredients of an industrial revolution were not present in pre-Civil War America and that the transcontinental railroads were highly desirable, citing Robert Fogel's estimates of the social returns from the railroad. Salsbury is particularly good at noting the inherent limitations of statistics to provide a definitive answer to these questions, but he holds out hope that future research might help answer them.

At this point it is worth noting that the Beards' claims are in serious theoretical doubt. The Republicans' economic philosophy was not true laissez-faire. In fact, their policy agenda was the opposite of laissez-faire in that it advocated special treatment for big business and a much larger role for the federal government. This can be seen in Republican policies to subsidize railroads, provide protective tariffs, and increase government debt and government control over money and banking as well as in their attitude toward labor. Their policies, such as the protective tariff and subsidies for big business, are now considered economically wasteful, and the rationales for such policies have been largely discredited and are now considered nothing more than special interests seeking a handout from the taxpayer through the government. Even if these policies were a net benefit for industry or caused upward movements in GDP calculations, it would not necessarily be viewed as good for the overall economy because it ignores the negative effects on the agriculture, service, and cultural sectors. The Republicans' policy would be better labeled as mercantilist in that it facilitated rent-seeking behavior.[7]

The transcontinental railroads are considered a great American success, and their completion from coast to coast marks the end of the period of Manifest Destiny and the beginning of American imperialism. While hailed as a triumph, the railroads themselves were highly corrupt operations and were not very profitable or desirable. Calculations of the "social results" of such projects are based on the notion of adding consumer surplus (value over price) to the roads' profits (price over cost) as well as more dubious notions such as the multiplier effect and the sentiment of "build it and they will come." Like war and natural disasters, the idea that subsidized railroads help the economy suffers from Bastiat's fallacy of the broken window because it emphasizes "what is seen" and ignores "what is not seen." Capital diverted to railroad building would surely have been put to good use elsewhere in the economy. If the roads had not been subsidized and taxpayers had simply spent their money on something else, they, too, would have created secondary effects and received consumer surplus from their purchases. Given that the railroads could practice price discrimination (charge higher prices to riders who received greater value), consumer surplus from these railroads would have been relatively low compared to alternative consumer purchases and investments. Moreover, had railroads not been highly subsidized, a better built, lower cost, and more timely system could have been put in place. For example, a central line connecting Kansas City with San Francisco (with connecting lines north and south at both end points) could have served the needs of transcontinental travel for a very long time and preserved a mountain of capital for other purposes. In addition, with only one major project in the West, the diversion of labor, wood, and iron would have been greatly diminished and available for other uses. This approach also would have had major repercussions for the Chinese immigrants who laid the track, for the Native American population who were displaced, and for the environment.

Tariffs were a centerpiece of Republican policy. They reversed a relatively free-trade policy and implemented the Morrill Tariff Bill in 1862, which raised the level of the tax on imports from roughly 20 percent to 50 percent, where it remained for the rest of the century. G. R. Hawke estimated that in 1889 the tariff provided twenty-one major industries with 100 percent protection against imports.[8] The implications of this policy were to provide higher sales, prices, and profits to those protected industries, which no doubt stimulated their development. On the down side, protectionism forced consumers to pay higher prices for both imported and domestically produced goods protected by the tariff—that is, they purchased fewer of these products, used less desirable substitutes, and had a lower standard of living. On net, the losses to consumers and the overall economy are greater than the gains to the protected producers and the tax revenue that accrues to the government.

Economists agree that protectionism is unambiguously bad for an economy, and they have disposed of all the arguments that have been used to support tariffs.[9] So while Republican policy certainly did shift development toward industry, it did so at the expense of agriculture and reduced the general standard of living from the level that could have otherwise been achieved. The notion that protectionism funneled capital and labor into industry is a one-sided argument. It neglects the fact that this capital and labor could have been put to more effective use in other areas of the economy to generate a higher standard of living (increased production and lower prices) and to enhance international trade and global economic development. According to Patrick O'Brien, there is no evidence that the tariff "promoted an allocation of resources that in the long run fostered higher levels of per capita income—even in the Northern states."[10] Note that this does not mean that industry would have disappeared had a free-trade policy been adopted, only that it would have been smaller, more efficient, and differently composed. For example, if protections on steel were removed, the domestic steel industry would have been smaller, but lower steel prices would have helped other industries such as railroads.

THE IMPACT OF THE WAR: THE ECONOMISTS' VIEW

While the old textbook view of the postwar period remains popular, historians and economic historians have become increasingly skeptical of the positive economic impact of the war. At a conference on the economic changes effected by the Civil War, the bulk of the evidence presented indicated that the war had a neutral to negative impact.[11] For example, in the opening lecture, George Rogers Taylor made the claim that economic growth continued after the conflict and that the war did not fundamentally affect the ongoing boom in the economy. Robert Sharkey analyzed all the changes in economic institutions and found that only in commercial banking was there a notable institutional alteration as a result of the war. Even here he was forced to admit that the dominance of demand deposits and the establishment of clearinghouses to facilitate exchange and prevent banking crises had already been in place before the war. Therefore, the only big changes directly attributable to the conflict were the huge increases in bank holdings of government debt securities during the war, the shift from state to national banks, and the shift toward favoring the interests of big-city banks in which the concerns of large-scale businesses were favored over small-scale businesses. Here, the East held financial power over the interests of the less well-developed regions to the South and West, all the direct result of the National Banking Act. He then concluded:

> As the National Banking System took shape after the War, it was apparent that human ingenuity would have had difficulty contriving a more perfect engine for class and sectional exploitation: creditors finally obtaining the upper hand as opposed to debtors, and the developed East holding the whip over the undeveloped West and South. This tipping of the class and sec-

tional balance of power was, in my opinion, *the* momentous change over the twenty-three-year period, 1850–1873.[12]

Banking, particularly in the South was harmed as a result of the war. The imperfect system of free banking and state-chartered banking was replaced with a system of national banks. As Robert Sharkey noted, "the seeds of decay had been planted. The National Banking System, with its yet unsuspected exploitative potentialities, had been established."[13] As a result, big business had better access to the money market, and small business was virtually shut out. Sharkey lamented, "Is it any wonder that the true advocates of free non-corporate enterprise such as Henry Carey screamed so unrestrainedly at what they called the 'money monopolists' of New York?"[14] Banks from New York City that charged high interest rates on loans made to the South were "another contributing factor to the decline of the pre-Civil War type of free enterprise."[15] The Republicans' system of national banking helped the robber barons to take over, and banking played a key role in this takeover.

One possible link between the Civil War and a booming postwar economy would be enhanced technology in terms of inventions as well as in innovations in business operations. However, there is not much evidence that the war enhanced technology, and there is a great deal of evidence that it actually hindered it. For example, Hunter Dupree found that the war did little in the way of spurring inventions. He noted that all of the basic national science institutions had already been started prior to the conflict and that the war stopped most of the military and science exploration teams that had begun their work during the 1850s.

One of the leading historians on applied research of this period, Robert Bruce, claimed that the "Civil War was not only not affected by applied science but also was itself a distinct detriment to basic science." Like Dupree, he noted that before the war the important science institutions were founded and most of the scientific principles were established, and that the war did not add to scientific or technological development. For example, the Gatling gun, or machine gun, was new but not put to much effective use. Indeed, most of the military technology was already in operation or on the shelf prior to the war. According to Dupree, "there wasn't much advancement in peaceful technology caused by the war."[16]

One notable historian of the late nineteenth-century American economy, Alfred Chandler, sought to challenge the negative view of the Civil War by examining developments in transportation and business organization, but he was forced to conclude that the conflict provided little or no benefits in these areas. He examined the factory for mass production of durable goods and the corporate form of business to control men and money. Large-scale businesses such as railroads, the telegraph, and the mail service required new forms of organization such as the corporation, which led to the growth of a large-scale finance operation on Wall Street. However, all of these businesses and the corporate form had already been developed prior to the war, and the National Banking Act had as much or more to do with the importance of Wall Street. Chandler therefore concluded: "If we take a broad perspective, then it seems safe to say that, of all the decades in the second half of the nineteenth century, the decade of the 1860s witnessed the fewest and least important changes in the organization of American transportation."[17]

The same conclusion may be reached in terms of manufacturing technology. Most of the important manufacturing technology, such as the use of interchangeable parts, was introduced prior to the war and was widely adopted in the 1850s. Chandler found that improvements in technology and innovations in business organization were actually much more apparent during the depression of the 1870s, when lower prices and competition forced entrepreneurial change, than during the so-called "prosperity" of the 1860s. Therefore, Chandler argued that "the Civil War appears to have had little impact on the organization of American transportation and manufacturing, particularly if viewed from the perspective of half a century's rapid development."[18]

More recently, research by Kenneth Sokoloff confirms that improvements in technology in manufacturing were already present to a significant degree in the antebellum economy. American business had achieved a high rate of growth in terms of technological improvements and a great deal of innovation in terms of manufacturing, product development, and organization prior to the war, giving rise at this time to the phrase, "Yankee ingenuity." (The existing evidence suggests that it was coined by Henry David Thoreau in 1843.) Sokoloff found that a "broad range of industries in the Northeast was able to realize substantial progress. Indeed, over the entire period from 1820–1860, the total productivity of capital and labor in manufacturing grew nearly as rapidly as after the Civil War and accounted for virtually all of the increase in labor productivity. Only in the 1850s did a second phase of technological development, characterized by mechanization and major increases in the capital intensity of production, spread beyond textiles to the rest of the sector."

Sokoloff writes that an "extraordinary expansion of markets . . . played a fundamental role in the achievement of these gains," and that these gains created a self-sustaining process of economic progress and economic growth that we would now call an industrial revolution. His evidence shows a two-stage process to this industrial revolution. In the first stage he finds evidence of invention and innovation during the early antebellum period, in the form of an increase in patents. In the second stage, patents aimed at more capital-intensive technologies and large-scale businesses were granted in areas similar to the first stage. This finding suggests that improvements in the second stage were dependent on improvements in the first stage, which in turn clearly demonstrates that postwar improvements were dependent on prewar ones. If anything, the war hindered or delayed postwar developments.[19]

Therefore, we find little evidence, either theoretical or otherwise, in the areas of the protective tariff, the national banking system, public works such as the intercontinental railroads, or innovative technology, that the Civil War contributed anything positive to postwar economic development. It remains to be seen, however, if the economy experienced high rates of economic growth and expansion.

ECONOMIC GROWTH

Central to the process of economic growth is the growth and development of the capital stock, which includes such things as buildings, machinery, and farmland. Economic historian Robert

Gallman, who was sympathetic to the notion that the war made a positive contribution to the economy, developed much of the evidence presented here.[20] According to Gallman, capital stock formation accelerated between 1774 and 1860, especially in the twenty years prior to the Civil War. Land clearings and farm breakings were a significant form of capital accumulation between 1800 and 1840, while nonagricultural capital greatly expanded between 1840 and 1860. Naturally, "the rate of growth of real national product per capita accelerated in the years before the Civil War" because it is savings and growth in the capital stock that generates higher productivity, wages, standards of living, and economic growth. Gallman's evidence may understate capital formation, especially in the earlier decades, and therefore overstate the rate of acceleration because the value of clearing farmland is based on historical wage rates for the labor needed to clear it, rather than on the value of the farmland itself. Also, much of the clearing of farmland was done in the off season when the opportunity cost of labor was less than wage rates.

In Table 4-1 we present Gallman's estimate for the conventional measure of the capital stock and his estimate of this conventional measure with the value of land clearings. We use an average of the capital price index and the consumer price index to derive the real or inflation-adjusted average annual rate of change over the various time periods.

Table 4-1. Inflation-Adjusted Capital Stock Formation, 1774–1980

Period	Conventional Concept (percent)	Including Farmland (percent)
1774–1799	.90	.25
1774–1840	1.05	.60
1799–1840	1.10	.75
1840–1860	2.95	2.40
1840–1900	2.30	1.85
1860–1900	2.05	1.65
1900–1929	1.80	na
1900–1980	1.60	na

Source: Adapted from Robert E. Gallman, "American Economic Growth before the Civil War: The Testimony of the Capital Stock Estimates," in *American Economic Growth and Standards of Living before the Civil War*, ed. Robert E. Gallman and John Joseph Wallis (Chicago: University of Chicago Press, 1992), 79–115. Reprinted by permission of the University of Chicago Press.

This evidence clearly suggests that the growth of the capital stock was accelerating from the years of the early Republic (less than 1 percent) to the late antebellum period (almost 3 percent) and then declined in the postwar period and into the twentieth century. Gallman's view is that "development consists of structural change"[21] and that "the structure of the capital stock changed very little, down to 1840. Thereafter, there were accelerating shifts,"[22] primarily a move from animals to structures. "There is the strong suggestion of an economy shifting in the direction of industrial activity and modern economic growth: away from agriculture and animal power, and toward manufacturing and mechanical power."[23] Economic growth in the early period was hampered by two major wars (the American Revolution and the War of 1812) and the Embargo of 1807. "The strong suggestion of these data is that the per capita supply of all inputs, taken together, must have grown very slowly, if at all, down to 1800, when it began to increase, the increase becoming more marked as time passed."[24]

Gallman's evidence here is essentially the same type that he presented in 1986. In that article, however, he made two relevant comments concerning the Civil War. First, he noted that the war had caused capital shallowing in the form of improved farmland in the South returning to its fallow state. He surmised, "One would think that the effects of the War on improved land would have been largely removed by 1875, but it may be that the value of improvements had not yet attained the level it would have reached had there been no war." We think a better explanation is that the effect of the war on improved land was removed by 1875 but that the Republicans' economic policy of deliberately favoring industry in the North at the expense of agriculture in the South was responsible for the continuing degradation of Southern farmland. Gallman also notes that the net claims on foreigners or foreign ownership of American capital were small or negative until 1860 but were very large in 1875, a result he attributes to the Civil War, "which increased the volume of negotiable American debt, altered the disposition of American savings, and changed the American balance of trade."[25]

The evidence of progress for antebellum labor shows that labor did well in terms of the size of the workforce, wages, per capita income, and wealth. Thomas Weiss shows the labor force and wage rates rising throughout the period. Real GDP per capita increased in every decade (using four different estimates) from 1800 through 1860.[26] Taking the average of his four different estimates of real Gross Domestic Product per capita gives us the following estimates for average annual growth from 1800 to 1860.[27] These estimates, shown in Table 4-2, clearly indicate that real per capita income is rising at an increasing rate.

Table 4-2. Rates of Real Per Capita Economic Growth, 1800–1860

Period	Average Annual Growth Rate* (percent)
1800–1820	.35
1820–1840	.79
1840–1860	1.20

*Average annual growth rate is measured as the annual percentage change in real (inflation adjusted) Gross Domestic Product per capita.
Source: Thomas Weiss, "U.S. Labor Force Estimates and Economic Growth, 1800–1860," in *American Economic Growth and Standards of Living before the Civil War*, ed. Robert E. Gallman and John Joseph Wallis (Chicago: University of Chicago Press, 1992), 27. Reprinted by permission of the University of Chicago Press.

Therefore the antebellum period was one of economic growth, where the rate of growth in income was rising at an increasing rate. This confirms and supports the evidence that the capital stock also experienced phenomenal growth in the antebellum period. Weiss argues:

> Even with this modest increase the economy of 1840 had clearly surpassed the achievements at the turn of the century, or that just prior to the Revolution. It was not quite the suddenly buoyant performance revealed in the conjectures of Paul David, but it was better than [those] pictured by earlier writers. George Taylor and Douglass North, along with Robert Martin, had clearly underestimated the economy's long-term performance and its ability to deal with misfortune and to recover from it. Even [Simon] Kuznets's suggestion that per capita output had increased by at least 19 percent between 1800 and 1840 was a bit pessimistic.[28]

It is also the case that there is no strong evidence of a general deterioration in the economic conditions of the "poor" and that "the benefits of growth were widely distributed, and income and wealth size distributions were fundamentally stable."[29] Confirming this observation, Kenneth Sokoloff and Georgia Villaflor examined the status of antebellum manufacturing workers and found: "It might seem remarkable, therefore, that the material benefits from the onset of growth in the American Northeast were widely shared and that all of the groups distinguishable in our data realized substantial increases in real wages over the period from 1820 to 1860."[30]

Labor markets in the antebellum period functioned in near textbook fashion. Labor was upwardly, geographically, and professionally mobile and there was almost no union or governmental restriction on the flow of labor resources. The result was that workingmen experienced higher incomes and standards of living over the period and that there was much less conflict between capital and labor in the antebellum period compared to the postbellum period.[31]

BLACK RECONSTRUCTION

There are many books about Reconstruction, especially about its more sensational aspects and politics. There are also many fine books about the economic aspects of the period. This section is drawn largely from the classic work by Robert Higgs and presents only the basic economic results of black Reconstruction.[32]

During and after the war, the black population suffered severe economic hardship, as did most Southerners. However, the evidence seems to indicate that they recovered rather quickly, despite dire predictions by many Southern and Northern whites that, once freed from slavery, the race would not survive. The number of blacks increased, but not at prewar rates, as they moved into urban areas. This decline in fertility was a normal capitalistic response to their newfound freedom, urbanization, and higher incomes, but many other factors could have played a role. Partially offsetting this decline in fertility (births) was a decline in mortality (deaths). The lower death rate was the result of higher income, which permitted purchases of better food, clothing, and shelter. Many of the black migrants went to the Northeast and Midwest in search of the higher-wage jobs in industry created by Republican economic policy. But the majority heeded the advice of black leaders such as Frederick Douglass and made the most of their economic opportunities in the South.

After the war ended, Republicans had no well-developed plans to care for the black population and to better establish them in the economy. The Freedmen's Bureau went inactive in 1869 and the Federal Army of Occupation left in 1877. There was no explicit land redistribution program or effective Homestead Act, so blacks were forced to make their own economic salvation. In fact, most of the land giveaways in the postbellum South went to wealthy Northerners.[33] To the surprise of most whites, from both the North and South, blacks were willing to work hard for good wages. Based on labor participation rates, blacks did work less than they had done under slavery. Women and children especially pursued more homemaking and education than before.

Naturally, the transition period from slavery to freedom, occurring as it did in the aftermath of the calamity and devastation of the war, was one of chaos and economic hardship. The Freedman's Bureau was incapable of fully dealing with the problems of the elderly, infirm, and orphaned blacks who previously had been the legal responsibility of their owners. There was also not a well-established legal framework that would protect people (particularly blacks) against crime and fraudulent contracts, and the Federal Army of Occupation was almost as likely to commit crimes as to enforce the law. The vacuum in the legal framework after the war caused immense suffering and forced people to devise their own solutions. The shared-rent system in which landowners and tenant farmers shared the crop (usually a 50-50 split depending on how much in capital goods the landowner provided) soon replaced the wage system in farming because it gave blacks (and some poor whites) a degree of independence and opportunity while minimizing interaction and conflict between the former slaves and their former masters. Over time, many black tenants were able to purchase their own small farms, despite a lack of capital and credit and the resentment and resistance of whites.

Many blacks moved into nonagricultural occupations where they had formerly worked as slaves. While many of these were menial jobs and many skilled ones were open to "whites only," blacks could achieve equal pay in jobs held by both blacks and whites. Given the catastrophic origins of their emancipation, the lack of any substantive support programs, and a discriminatory legal and governmental structure, the progress achieved in the years after the war by former slaves was substantial, if not remarkable.

Toward the end of the century black farmers increasingly entered into fixed-share tenancy contracts with landowners. This contract provided blacks with greater independence and profit opportunities. The increased risks inherent in the fixed-share contract was a reflection that these blacks had proven themselves skilled and experienced farm managers in the eyes of landowners as well as their own. The terms of contracts also improved because blacks had accumulated their own capital goods such as mules, horses, and plows. Land ownership also continued to expand for blacks. In Georgia, black ownership increased from 587,000 acres in 1880 to 1,608,000 acres in 1910 despite a severe depression in cotton prices between 1892 and 1900.[34]

Blacks were able to enter unskilled jobs and receive comparable wages, but they had great difficulty in entering skilled labor markets because they were untrained. Black trade schools, such as the Tuskegee Institute, were a source of insignificant numbers of industrial workers because their emphasis was on the training of teachers who would educate future generations. Perhaps the biggest obstacle was the trade unions, especially in the North. Unions tried to keep blacks out of high-paying jobs and to maintain (largely unsuccessfully) discriminatory wage rates, although blacks often served as effective strikebreakers. Black leaders considered labor unions to be the enemy of the black workingman.[35]

As blacks established themselves in the economy and began to advance, the government increasingly tried to stymie their progress. Jim Crow laws, disenfranchisement, public segregation laws, and the *Plessy v. Ferguson* (1896) decision of the Supreme Court all undercut the economic development of the black population, while law enforcement failed to protect blacks against lynching, white terrorism, and union violence. In the attempt to shelter themselves from all this abuse, blacks turned to "group economy," but this effort at self-protection also greatly limited their economic opportunities.

Data do not exist for good income estimates, but Robert Higgs figured that black income increased anywhere from 100 to 400 percent from the Civil War to 1900.[36] This growth rate in black income exceeded that of whites, but its level remained below that of whites by a substantial amount. The evidence available indicates that most blacks not only could provide for food, clothing, and shelter but also had some discretionary income for the purchase of "nonessentials" such as alcohol, tobacco, musical instruments, and Bibles. At the beginning of the twentieth century, blacks were relatively poor compared to the white population and severely poor compared to modern Americans, but in spite of their desperate circumstances, little support, and an often-hostile white population and government, they made tremendous progress in improving their standard of living.

LINCOLN AND THE FIRST NEW DEAL

Most important from a moral perspective, the Civil War resulted in the emancipation of the slave population. Slavery was not only a central cause of the war but it was also a cardinal element in its outcome. It prevented the European intervention that was vital to the Southern economy and it forced the Confederacy into the costly military strategy of a rigid peripheral defense with large standing armies.

An economic rather than a moral reason for both secession and war was the ambitious economic agenda of the Republican Party—an agenda similar to that of Alexander Hamilton and Whig leader Henry Clay, which involved protective tariffs, national banks, public works, and plenty of patronage. The Southern states bolted from the Republic because they knew they would be economically harmed by these policies and could reap an economic advantage with independence. Although we have shown that the Southerners' *practice* was different during the war, their *ideology* of free trade, sound money, states' rights, and limited government was also based on their economic self-interest. This ideology formed the grounds for the changes they made to the Constitution to prevent protectionism, limit government, and discourage special privilege through government.[37] The defeat of the Confederacy was therefore an ideological downfall for the cause of anti-Federalist, Jeffersonian, and Jacksonian traditions of small, limited government while the changes to the Constitution (the Thirteenth, Fourteenth, and Fifteenth Amendments) are now considered essential to the centralization of government power over individual and states' rights.

The flurry of new laws, regulations, and bureaucracies created by President Lincoln and the Republican Party is reminiscent of Franklin Roosevelt's New Deal in the 1930s, for the volume, scope, and questionable constitutionality of its legislative output. However, although Roosevelt followed Lincoln, it should not be too surprising to learn that the term "New Deal" was actually coined in March 1865 by a newspaper editor in Raleigh to characterize Lincoln and the Republicans and persuade North Carolina voters to rejoin the Union. The massive expansion of the federal government into the economy led Daniel Elazar to claim that "one could easily call Lincoln's presidency the 'New Deal' of the 1860s."[38] Among the major elements of Lincoln's New Deal, cited by Elazar, are the following:

Morrill Tariff (1861)
First Income Tax (1861)
Expanded Postal Service (1861)
Homestead Act (1862)
Morrill Land-Grant College Act (1862)
Department of Agriculture (1862)
Bureau of Printing and Engraving (1862)
Transcontinental Railroad land grants (1862, 1863, 1864)
National Banking Acts (1863, 1864, 1865, 1866)
Comptroller of the Currency (1863)
National Academy of Science (1863)
Free urban mail delivery (1863)
Yosemite nature reserve land grant (1864)
Contract Labor Act (1864)
Office of Immigration (1864)
Railway mail service (1864)
Money order system (1864)

There are three significant ways in which Lincoln's New Deal and the Civil War can be characterized. First, the Civil War certainly represents the first and most important increase in the size and scope of the national government. Robert Higgs has developed a model of growth in which national crises serve to "ratchet up" the size of the government. During the crisis the government grows by leaps and bounds and afterward shrinks, but it does not fall back to the precrisis levels of authority, power, and spending. In his theoretical model it is the crisis of war, depression, social conflict, and "rampant terrorism" that causes big government and the destruction of individual liberty and the free society. While Higgs begins his analysis in 1893, he does label the Civil War explicitly as *the* crisis of the nineteenth century that "challenged America's political and economic order so profoundly."[39] The Civil War and Lincoln's New Deal therefore can be characterized as one of the first and most important episodes in the growth of government.

The second economic characterization of the war and Lincoln's New Deal is given by Richard Bensel, who, in *Yankee Leviathan*, offers a sophisticated and comprehensive class and interest-group analysis of the Civil War. Bensel shows in great detail how the war is really the origin of central state authority in America, and he describes the classes who benefited from the dramatic changes in American political economy. The book is particularly useful in terms of understanding how the Union and Confederacy mobilized for the war effort. Bensel notes the irony that the big-government Republicans actually relied heavily on the market process to mobilize their war efforts, whereas the limited-government Confederates resorted to comprehensive government control of the economy to fight the war.[40] It is likely, moreover, that such Southern practices (such as to centralize trade controls during the war) were motivated by their desire to preserve the institution of slavery and to defend other economic interests.

The third and final way in which to characterize Lincoln's New Deal in terms of economic theory is to label the Republican economic agenda as mercantilist. An early school of economic thought, the mercantilists promoted business interests with policies such as protectionism, paper money and easy credit, monopolies, subsidies, public works, and colonialism. This school was thoroughly discredited by classical economists such as Adam

Smith, David Ricardo, and Karl Marx. Recent research shows that mercantilists should not be characterized as serious students of scientific inquiry, but rather as an early form of lobbyists. Mercantilist regimes were not promoting general economic health but were *rent-seeking societies* where interest groups lobbied governments for special privileges such as monopolies, protection from international trade, and government contracts.[41] In addition to following the typical mercantilist economic policies, the massive corruption that ensued after the war supports the contention that the Republican reign could aptly be characterized as a rent-seeking society.

Thus, interest-group analysis and economics help to explain not only the factors associated with the Civil War but also how profitability associated with such interest-group activities created the strong, centralized regulatory economy that exists in the United States today. To be sure, the latter story is a long one. Two World Wars, "progressivism," the Great Depression and Roosevelt's New Deal, the Cold War, and Vietnam all had a great impact on shaping the modern mega-national government. But the Civil War was the watershed event in altering the form of government that the ideology and institutions of the American Revolution and the U.S. Constitution had maintained up to that time. Economic theory and interest-group analysis have much to contribute to our understanding of the Civil War.

NOTES

1. Ludwig von Mises, *Nation, State, and Economy: Contributions to the Politics and History of Our Time*, trans. Leland B. Yeager (New York: New York University Press, 1983), 153.
2. Frédéric Bastiat, "What Is Seen and What Is Not Seen," in *Selected Essays on Political Economy* (Princeton, NJ: D. Van Nostrand Company, [1850] 1964).
3. Robert Higgs, "Wartime Prosperity? A Reassessment of the U.S. Economy in the 1940s," *Journal of Economic History* 52 (March 1992): 41–60.
4. Llewellyn Rockwell, "Hurricane Economics," Daily Article on Mises.org, September 22, 1999.
5. Mancur Olson, *The Rise and Decline of Nations: Economic Growth, Stagflation, and Social Rigidities* (New Haven: Yale University Press, 1982).
6. Thomas Cochran, "Did the Civil War Retard Industrialization?" *Mississippi Valley Historical Review* 48 (September 1961): 197–210.

102   TARIFFS, BLOCKADES, AND INFLATION

7. Robert B. Ekelund Jr. and Robert Tollison, *Mercantilism as a Rent-Seeking Society* (College Station: Texas A&M University Press, 1981).

8. G. R. Hawke, "The United States Tariff and Industrial Protection in the Late Nineteenth Century," *Economic History Review* 28 (February 1975): 84–99.

9. Arvind Panagariya, "Cost of Protection: Where Do We Stand?" *American Economic Review* 92 (May 2002): 175–79.

10. Patrick O'Brien, *The Economic Effects of the American Civil War* (Atlantic Highlands, NJ: Humanities Press International, 1988), 67.

11. *Economic Change in the Civil War Era: Proceedings of a Conference on American Economic Institutional Change, 1850–1873, and the Impact of the Civil War Held March 12–14, 1964* (hereafter *Economic Change*), ed. David T. Gilchrist and W. David Lewis (Greenville, DE: Eleutherian Mills-Hagley Foundation, 1965).

12. Robert P. Sharkey, "Commercial Banking," in *Economic Change*, 27.

13. Ibid., 30.

14. Ibid., 31.

15. Ibid.

16. Robert V. Bruce, "Science and Technology," in *Economic Change*, 124.

17. Alfred D. Chandler Jr., "The Organization of Manufacturing and Transportation," in *Economic Change*, 147.

18. Ibid., 148.

19. Kenneth L. Sokoloff, "Invention, Innovation, and Manufacturing Productivity Growth in the Antebellum Northeast," in *American Economic Growth and Standards of Living before the Civil War* (hereafter *American Economic Growth*), ed. Robert E. Gallman and John Joseph Wallis (Chicago: University of Chicago Press, 1992), 345–84.

20. Robert E. Gallman, "American Economic Growth before the Civil War: The Testimony of the Capital Stock Estimates," in *American Economic Growth*, 79–115.

21. Ibid., 92.

22. Ibid., 93.

23. Ibid.

24. Ibid., 96. See Gallman's Table 2.10, p. 97, which shows the rates of growth of the factors of production (per capita) for all periods: progression to 1860, and then decline to 1900.

25. Robert E. Gallman, "The United States Capital Stock in the Nineteenth Century," in Stanley L. Engerman and Robert E. Gallman, eds., *Long-Term Factors in American Economic Growth* (Chicago: University of Chicago Press, 1986), 165–213, see esp. 194.

26. Thomas Weiss, "U.S. Labor Force Estimates and Economic Growth, 1800–1860," in *American Economic Growth*, 19–75.

27. Ibid., Table 1.2, p. 27.

28. Ibid., 35.

29. Robert E. Gallman and John Joseph Wallis, "Introduction," in *American Economic Growth*, 5.

30. Kenneth L. Sokoloff and Georgia C. Villaflor, "The Market for Manufacturing Workers," in *Strategic Factors in Nineteenth-Century Ameri-*

can Economic History: A Volume to Honor Robert W. Fogel, ed. Claudia Goldin and Hugh Rockoff (Chicago: University of Chicago Press, 1992), 29–65.

31. Robert Margo, *Wages and Labor Markets in the United States, 1820–1860* (Chicago: University of Chicago Press, 2000).

32. Robert Higgs, *Competition and Coercion: Blacks in the American Economy, 1865–1914* (New York: Cambridge University Press, 1977).

33. Paul Wallace Gates, "Federal Land Policy in the South, 1866–1888," *Journal of Southern History* 6 (August 1940): 303–30.

34. Higgs, *Competition and Coercion*, 69.

35. Ibid., 86.

36. Ibid., 102.

37. Marshall L. DeRosa, *The Confederate Constitution of 1861: An Inquiry into American Constitutionalism* (Columbia: University of Missouri Press, 1991).

38. Daniel J. Elazar, "Comment," in *Economic Change*, 94–108, esp. 98–99.

39. Robert Higgs, *Crisis and Leviathan: Critical Episodes in the Growth of American Government* (New York: Oxford University Press, 1987), 262, 77.

40. Richard Franklin Bensel, *Yankee Leviathan: The Origins of Central State Authority in America, 1859–1877* (New York: Cambridge University Press, 1990). Also see Karl Marx and Freidrich Engels, *The Civil War in the United States* (1861), for a perceptive analysis of the war based on their reading of British newspapers and journals. They concluded, "The war between the North and the South is a tariff war. The war is, further, not for any principle, does not touch the question of slavery, and in fact turns on the Northern lust for sovereignty," p. 58 (New York: International Publishers, 1937).

41. Robert B. Ekelund Jr. and Robert Tollison, *Politicized Economies: Monarchy, Monopoly, and Mercantilism* (College Station: Texas A&M University Press, 1997).

BIBLIOGRAPHICAL ESSAY

In the longer run, most historic events become relatively less important in our lives and sometimes drop out of our memory altogether. Such is not the case with the American Civil War. In the post-World War II period, the Civil War has become almost a fixture of everyday life in America. Plays, movies, and television specials about the war are popular entertainment; tourists flock to battlefields and monuments; magazines, books (both fact and fiction), paintings and artifacts sell like hotcakes; events and battles of the war are reenacted; and even political disputes regarding the use of historic battlefields and the Confederate battleflag testify to our enduring interest in the Civil War and the importance of understanding its full meaning. Economists have also demonstrated a growing concern with the war and with the economic issues of that period. Some highlights of the economics of the Civil War are presented here, with special emphasis on those items not explicitly referenced or explained in the text, as well as the newer literature on the subject.

One of the best books for general coverage of the economics of the war is Jeffrey Rogers Hummel, *Emancipating Slaves, Enslaving Free Men: A History of the American Civil War* (Chicago: Open Court, 1996). It is comprehensive in scope, and Hummel brings together the complete breadth of historical literature of the Civil War era and a thorough knowledge and understanding of economic theory. Another very important book is David Surdam, *Northern Naval Superiority and the Economics of the American Civil War* (Columbia: University of South Carolina Press, 2001), in which the economic effects of the Union blockade are examined in comprehensive and microscopic detail. It shows the full ramifications of the blockade on the Confederate war effort and breaks fresh ground in doing so. Surdam demonstrates empirically that the blockade did its damage primarily by preventing the usual

flow of cotton and, more provocatively, by disrupting both foreign and domestic trade within the South. As the transportation
of cotton and other goods had to rely more on the railroads, this
railroad commerce competed with military demands and thus
wore out the rails and locomotives faster. They could not be easily replaced, of course, because of the blockade. The book is a
strong antidote for those who view the blockade as a peripheral
issue. Roger L. Ransom's *Conflict and Compromise: The Political
Economy of Slavery, Emancipation, and the American Civil War* (New
York: Cambridge University Press, 1989) is a classic in the field,
while Ralph Andreano's collection of early articles and statistics,
The Economic Impact of the American Civil War (Cambridge, MA:
Schenkman, 1962), is a great source of material. Patrick O'Brien's
short book, *The Economic Effects of the American Civil War* (Atlantic Highlands, NJ: Humanities Press International, 1988), is a cost-
benefit analysis that finds the war politically successful but, in
purely material terms, unprofitable. Karl Marx and Friedrich
Engels provide an interesting and contemporaneous account in
The Civil War in the United States (New York: International Publishers, 1937).

The economic analysis of the Civil War has taken a decidedly
libertarian turn in recent years, the strength of which might be
based on the fact that the war itself was fought at the end of a
period in American history dominated by libertarian philosophy
as shown in James McPherson, *For Cause and Comrades: Why Men
Fought the Civil War* (New York: Oxford University Press, 1997).
See especially Thomas J. Pressly, " 'Emancipating Slaves, Enslaving Free Men': Modern Libertarians Interpret the United States
Civil War, 1960s–1990s: A Review Essay," *Civil War History* 46 (September 2000): 254–65. For an early and clear, if not radical, state-
ment of the libertarian perspective see Joseph R. Stromberg, "The
War for Southern Independence: A Radical Libertarian Perspective," *Journal of Libertarian Studies* 3, no. 1 (1979): 31–53.

SLAVERY

During the late Vietnam War era, government research grants
allowed Robert W. Fogel and Stanley L. Engerman to amass large
amounts of data on antebellum slavery, which they used to virtu-

ally rewrite the history of black slavery in America. Their book, *Time on the Cross* (Boston: Little, Brown, 1974), along with supplements, articles, and additional books, ignited the biggest of academic disputes that spanned several disciplines. Despite withering criticism from historians and economists alike on virtually every issue of fact and interpretation in their book, they were successful in deposing the traditional interpretation of slavery, which was based largely on the work of historians such as Ulrich Bonnell Phillips, *Negro Slavery: A Survey of the Supply, Employment, and Control of Negro Labor as Determined by the Plantation Regime* (New York: D. Appleton, 1918); Charles Ramsdell, "The Natural Limits of Slavery Expansion," *Mississippi Valley Historical Review* 16 (September 1929): 151–71; and Eugene D. Genovese, *The Political Economy of Slavery: Studies in the Economy and Society of the Slave South* (New York: Pantheon Books, 1965) and their students.

In the traditional view, slavery was not a vibrant economic institution on the eve of the Civil War. It had reached the limits of speculation, viable agricultural land, and political support and was doomed to stagnation, collapse, and possibly extinction. Fogel and Engerman, along with Kenneth M. Stampp's *The Peculiar Institution: Slavery in the Ante-Bellum South* (New York: Alfred A. Knopf, 1956), show slavery to be a profitable institution that was growing and expanding and unlikely to disappear for the foreseeable future. Obviously, this debate weighs on the subject of the Civil War: its various causes are intertwined with slavery and because the war resulted in emancipation, a tremendously important achievement if slavery was economically viable, or a minor attainment if slavery was on the verge of collapse. Modern mainstream economists have generally accepted Fogel and Engerman's findings because they tend to "let the numbers speak for themselves." In the aftermath of such damning criticism, it is less clear why historians have come to support the Stampp-Fogel-Engerman view, but in the last twenty-five years it has become the generally accepted one.

This result is somewhat unsettling given the stance of economists, at least from the time of Adam Smith over 225 years ago, that slavery is an inefficient form of labor supply. In fact, John Ruskin and Thomas Carlyle dubbed economics "the dismal science" because nineteenth-century classical economists such as

John Stuart Mill and John Cairnes were the leading voices against slavery and the supporters of self-government for the common man *and woman*, a long-forgotten point recently rediscovered in David Levy's unorthodox book, *How the Dismal Science Got Its Name: Classical Economics and UR Text of Radical Politics* (Ann Arbor: University of Michigan Press, 2001). Modern examples of the classical or traditional economic approach to slavery can be found in Ludwig von Mises, "The Work of Animals and Slaves," in *Human Action: A Treatise on Economics*, 3d ed. (Chicago: Regnery, 1966); Murray N. Rothbard, "A Note on the Economics of Slavery" (May [approx.] 1960, 6 pgs.), The Murray N. Rothbard Papers, Ludwig von Mises Institute, Auburn, Alabama; Gordon Tullock, "The Political Economy of Slavery," *Left and Right* 3 (Spring–Summer 1967): 5–16; and Thomas Sowell, *Markets and Minorities* (New York: Basic Books, 1981).

The Fogel and Engerman thesis is reviewed, along with most of their critics from the perspectives of the Classical and Austrian Schools of economics, in Mark Thornton, "Slavery, Profitability, and the Market Process," *Review of Austrian Economics* 7 (1994): 21–47 [http://www.mises.org/journals/rae/pdf/rae7 2 2.pdf]. Slavery is shown here to be inconsistent with the market process. For a more up-to-date listing of references and a review of the entire history of economic thought related to slavery see Mark A. Yanochik, "Essays on the Economics of Slavery" (Ph.D. dissertation, Auburn University, 1997). Yanochik also presents modern applications of the Classical-Austrian view of slavery that emphasizes the need for government intervention to ensure the sustainability of the institution. This "new" perspective on the economics of slavery emphasizes the role of public policy in sustaining slavery. See especially Mark A. Yanochik, Bradley T. Ewing, and Mark Thornton, "A New Perspective on Antebellum Slavery: Public Policy and Slave Prices," *Atlantic Economic Journal* 29 (September 2001): 330–40, and Mark A. Yanochik, Mark Thornton, and Bradley T. Ewing, "Railroad Construction and Slave Prices," *Social Science Quarterly* 84, no. 3 (September 2003); and Mark Thornton and Mark A. Yanochik, "Did Slavery Pay?" *History in Dispute*, vol. 13, *History of Slavery in the Western Hemisphere, circa 1500–1888*, edited by Mark Malvasi (Columbia, SC: Manly Inc./Farmington Hills, MI: St. James Press, 2003). For a

complete description of this approach to slavery see Jeffrey Rogers
Hummel, "Deadweight Loss and the American Civil War: The
Political Economy of Slavery, Secession, and Emancipation" (Ph.D.
dissertation, University of Texas, 2001).
Most important, this literature provides reconciliation between the traditional historians and the new economic historians, or cliometricians. Slavery is shown to be uneconomical, as
the traditional historians claimed; but it gave the appearance of
viability and profitability because of government intervention on
behalf of slave owners that propped up the slave labor system,
socialized many of the important costs of ownership, directly
stimulated the productivity of slavery, and increased the income
and wealth of owners. We now have, for example, a specific explanation of the boom in slave prices of the 1850s (a subsidized
boom in railroad construction), which the traditional view attributed to the general irrationality of slave owners, and which the
new economic historians attributed to the general productivity
of slavery.

SECESSION AND WAR

For a good general treatment of the topic of secession, including the Confederacy, see *Secession, State, and Liberty* (New
Brunswick, NJ: Transaction Publishers, 1998), edited and introduced by David Gordon; and for an overview and general treatment of the history of American wars from an economic
perspective see *The Costs of War* (New Brunswick, NJ: Transaction Publishers, 1997), edited and introduced by John V. Denson.
See Ludwig von Mises, *Nation, State, and Economy: Contributions
to the Politics and History of Our Time* (New York: New York University Press, 1983), translated by Leland B. Yeager, for details
concerning the economic analysis of secession and war.
One topic of recent interest has been the writing of the Confederate Constitution and what it might reveal about the causes
and meaning of the Civil War. The Confederates essentially edited the U.S. Constitution in the areas of slavery and political
economy, and that editing could potentially tell us a great deal
about why the Confederate states left the Union. Marshall L. DeRosa,
The Confederate Constitution of 1861: An Inquiry into American

Constitutionalism (Columbia: University of Missouri Press, 1991), is the classic in the field, while Randall Holcombe, "The Distributive Model of Government: Evidence from the Confederate Constitution," *Southern Economic Journal* 58 (January 1992): 762–69, and Robert A. McGuire and T. Norman van Cott, "The Confederate Constitution, Tariffs, and the Laffer Relationship," *Economic Inquiry* 40 (July 2002): 428–34, examine the changes from the viewpoints of economics and public choice theory.

For recent controversial perspectives on the origins of secession and war see McPherson, *For Cause and Comrades*; Charles Adams, *When in the Course of Human Events: Arguing the Case for Southern Secession* (Lanham, MD: Rowman and Littlefield, 2000); and Thomas DiLorenzo, *The Real Lincoln* (Roseville, CA: Prima Publishing, 2002).

THE BLOCKADE

Did the Confederacy have a powerful economic weapon in its dominant position in the world cotton market? Was the blockade important, after all? This debate is presented and empirically simulated in David Surdam, "King Cotton: Monarch or Pretender? The State of the Market for Raw Cotton on the Eve of the American Civil War," *Economic History Review* 51 (February 1998): 113–32. Surdam argues here and in *Northern Naval Superiority* that the Confederacy could have used its market power or monopoly in cotton to obtain the revenues necessary to build an effective navy while simultaneously releasing enough labor to fight the land war. While Surdam argues that the South's informal embargo on cotton sales to Europe was a misguided policy, Stanley Lebergott makes the case that a more effective embargo was possibly the key to the Confederate victory in "Why the South Lost: Commercial Purposes in the Confederacy, 1861–1865," *Journal of American History* 70 (June 1983): 58–74. He has also argued that blockade-running was more expensive and less profitable than was previously thought and that most ships only attempted to run the blockade once; see "Through the Blockade: The Profitability and Extent of Cotton Smuggling, 1861–1865," *Journal of Economic History* 41 (December 1981): 867–88.

We tend to believe that either policy could have possibly worked had it been fully and effectively implemented, but we found Confederate policies to be both inconsistent and counterproductive in Robert B. Ekelund Jr., John D. Jackson, and Mark Thornton, "The 'Unintended Consequences' of Confederate Trade Legislation," *Eastern Economic Journal* (forthcoming in 2004); Robert B. Ekelund Jr. and Mark Thornton, "The Confederate Blockade of the South," *Quarterly Journal of Austrian Economics* 3 (Spring 2001): 23–42; and Robert B. Ekelund Jr. and Mark Thornton, "The Union Blockade versus Demoralization of the South: Relative Prices in the Confederacy," *Social Science Quarterly* 73 (December 1992): 890–902. Among other factors, Confederate policies added to the already high costs of running the blockade as described by Lebergott, and the lack of an effective Confederate navy (à la Surdam) made blockade-running much more expensive and ultimately crushed the Southern economy as well as the Confederate war effort.

MONEY AND BANKING

For an explanation of the theory of free banking and its stability see Lawrence H. White, *Free Banking in Britain: Theory, Experience, and Debate, 1800–1845* (New York: Cambridge University Press, 1984); George Selgin, *The Theory of Free Banking: A Study of the Supply of Money under Competitive Note Issue* (Lanham, MD: Rowman and Littlefield, 1988); Lawrence H. White, *Competition and Currency: Essays on Free Banking and Money* (New York: New York University Press, 1989); and Larry Sechrest, *Free Banking: Theory, History, and a Laissez-Faire Model* (Westport, CT: Quorum Books, 1993).

Hugh Rockoff provides the standard definition of wildcat banking and begins the reexamination of the phenomenon in "The Free Banking Era: A Reexamination," *Journal of Money, Credit, and Banking* 6 (May 1974): 141–67. Arthur J. Rolnick and Warren E. Weber show that free banking was not an economic problem and that wildcat banking was extremely limited and not socially harmful in "New Evidence on the Free Banking Era," *American Economic Review* 73 (December 1983): 1080–91. Gary Gorton explains in "Reputation Formation in Early Bank Note Markets," *Journal of Political Economy* 104 (April 1996): 346–97, that the role of bank reputation explains why privately issued money during the Free Banking Era was not plagued by problems of wildcat banking. For a description of the substantial role that banks played in financing state government see Richard Sylla, John B. Legler, and John J. Wallis, "Banks and State Public Finance in the New Republic: The United States, 1790–1860," *Journal of Economic History* 47 (June 1987): 391–403. For a description of some of the nineteenth-century bank panics in America see Charles DeLorme, Robert B. Ekelund Jr., and Mark Thornton, "The Anatomy of Financial Panics: American Historical Episodes," *International Review of Economics and Business* 40 (October–November 1993): 915–30.

An interest in and exploration of Civil War monetary issues seem to be growing rather than waning over time. See, for example, Gary M. Pecquet, "Money in the Trans-Mississippi Confederacy and the Confederate Currency Reform Act of 1864," *Explorations in Economic History* 24 (April 1987): 218–43; Richard C. K. Burdekin and Farrokh K. Langdana, "War Finance in the Southern Confederacy, 1861–1865," *Explorations in Economic History* 30 (July 1993): 352–56; T. McCandless Jr., "Money, Expectations, and the U.S. Civil War," *American Economic Review* 86 (June 1996): 661–71; Kristen L. Willard, Timothy W. Guinnane, and Harvey S. Rosen, "Turning Points in the Civil War: Views from the Greenback Market," *American Economic Review* 86 (September 1996): 1001–18; William O. Brown Jr. and Richard C. K. Burdekin, "Turning Points in the U.S. Civil War: A British Perspective," *Journal of Economic History* 60 (March 2000): 216–31; Gary Pecquet, George Davis, and Bryce Kanago, "Confederate Money, Southern Expectations, and the National Bank Act during the Civil War: Evidence from Southern Bank Notes," Working Paper, May 2001; and Marc D. Weidenmier, "Turning Points in the U.S. Civil War: Views from the Grayback Market," *Southern Economic Journal* 68, no. 4 (April 2002): 875–90. In "Inflation Is Always and Everywhere a Monetary Phenomenon: Richmond vs. Houston in 1864," *American Economic Review* 91 (December 2001): 1621–30, Richard C. K. Burdekin and Marc D. Weidenmier reexamine Milton Friedman's Monetarist position from the body of research on monetary experience of the Civil War using the "natural experiment" of the Confederate Currency Reform Act of 1864, in which a new revalued currency was issued and exchanged in the eastern Confederacy but not west of the Mississippi until late in the war. Their evidence clearly shows that "war news" was not the whole story and that changes in the quantity of money were more in line with price inflation than previously thought. George Selgin, "The Suppression of State Banknotes: A Reconsideration," *Economic Inquiry* 38 (October 2000): 600–615, finds that the true purpose or effect of the tax on state bank notes was not to enhance bond sales or to improve the quality of the currency but rather to reduce the inflationary effects of greenbacks and national bank notes. According to Selgin, over the long run this was more harmful to the general public than had state banks continued to issue their own currency.

TRUTH AND CONSEQUENCES

Does war help the economy? Evidence continues to build that the opposite is the case. See, for example, Lee A. Craig and Thomas Weiss, "Agricultural Productivity Growth during the Decade of the Civil War," *Journal of Economic History* 53 (September 1993): 527–48. They found that the increase in agricultural production was not the result of improved productivity but rather from putting more women and children in the fields for longer hours. An important contribution against the notion of "build it and they will come" and the public infrastructure argument is Robert W. Fogel, *The Union Pacific Railroad: A Case of Premature Enterprise* (Baltimore, MD: Johns Hopkins University Press, 1969). Stanley L. Engerman, "The Economic Impact of the Civil War," in *The Reinterpretation of American Economic History*, edited by Robert W. Fogel and Stanley L. Engerman (New York: Harper and Row, 1971), convincingly shows that the Civil War was not good for the economy.

For a good example of economic hardship in the postwar South see Garland Brinkley, "The Decline in Southern Agricultural Output, 1860–1880," *Journal of Economic History* 57 (March 1997): 116–38, who shows that there was a sharp decline in agricultural output and a rise in disease (hookworm), but that increased sharecropping actually spurred productivity. For a full treatment of the role of sharecropping see Lee J. Alston and Robert Higgs, "Contractual Mix in Southern Agriculture since the Civil War: Facts, Hypothesis, and Tests," *Journal of Economic History* 42 (June 1982): 327–53. Also see the earlier analyses of Roger L. Ransom and Richard Sutch, "Debt Peonage in the Cotton South after the Civil War," *Journal of Economic History* 32 (September 1972): 641–69; and by the same authors, "The Impact of the Civil War and of Emancipation on Southern Agriculture," *Explorations in Economic History* 12 (January 1975): 1–28. Peter Temin examined "The Post-Bellum Recovery of the South and the Cost of the Civil War," *Journal of Economic History* 36 (December 1976): 898–907, as did Claudia Dale Goldin and Frank D. Lewis, "The Economic Cost of the American Civil War: Estimates and Implications," *Journal of Economic History* 35 (June 1975): 299–326.

In terms of postwar institutions, the powerful role of the railroads is exposed by Scott Reynolds Nelson in *Iron Confederacies: Southern Railways, Klan Violence, and Reconstruction* (Chapel Hill: University of North Carolina Press, 1999). David Brian Robertson provides a recent history of the development of unions in *Capital, Labor, and State: The Battle for American Labor Markets from the Civil War to the New Deal* (Lanham, MD: Rowman and Littlefield, 2000). For postwar monetary institutions see William J. Laird and James R. Rinehart, "Deflation, Agriculture, and Southern Development," *Agricultural History* 42 (April 1968): 115–45; and John A. James, "Financial Underdevelopment in the Postbellum South," *Journal of Interdisciplinary History* 11 (Winter 1981): 443–54.

RECONSTRUCTION AND RACISM

Heather Cox Richardson has produced two recent books on the Civil War and Reconstruction. In *The Greatest Nation on the Earth: Republican Economic Policies during the Civil War* (Cambridge, MA: Harvard University Press, 1997), she explores how ideology influenced Union economic policy during the war. In her second book, *The Death of Reconstruction: Race, Labor, and Politics in the Post-Civil War North, 1865–1901* (Cambridge, MA: Harvard University Press, 2001), Richardson examines the North's abandonment of blacks after the war. Using newspaper accounts to go beyond a "race" explanation, she finds a key change in ideology and the dominant political economy of the nation. Prior to the war, Americans tended to hold a view of political economy in which labor and capital worked together in harmony (as might be reflected in the works of Frédéric Bastiat, the great French political economist who wrote extensively during the late 1840s). After the war, Richardson finds a sea change in ideology whereby labor and capital are now generally viewed as in conflict. This was also a time of increasing tension between creditor and debtor, capitalist and labor, and industry and agriculture as well as of the increasing use of political means to achieve economic ends. This system of progressive conflict eventually turned to blacks as both a source and a scapegoat for the war.

Jennifer Roback's "Southern Labor Law in the Jim Crow Era: Exploitative or Competitive?" *University of Chicago Law Review* 51 (Fall 1984): 1161–1192, showed how state power was used to uphold segregation. In "The Political Economy of Segregation: The Case of Segregated Streetcars," *Journal of Economic History* 46, no. 4 (December 1986): 893–917, Roback noted how state power stopped the otherwise integrative force of the free marketplace.

For an economic history of the black experience since emancipation see Roger L. Ransom and Richard Sutch, *One Kind of Freedom: The Economic Consequences of Emancipation* (New York: Cambridge University Press, 1977), and Jay R. Mandle, *Not Free, Not Slave: The African American Economic Experience since the Civil War* (Durham, NC: Duke University Press, 1992). For further references on the occurrence and theory of economic discrimination against blacks see William H. Hutt, *The Economics of the Colour Bar: A Study of the Economic Origins and Consequences of Racial Segregation in South Africa* (London: Institute of Economic Affairs, 1965); Walter Williams, *The State against Blacks* (New York: McGraw-Hill, 1982); and Thomas Sowell, *Markets and Minorities* (New York: Basic Books, 1981). See Leon F. Litwack, *North of Slavery: The Negro in the Free States, 1790–1860* (Chicago: University of Chicago Press, 1961), for details regarding the black legal codes in the north.

GROWTH OF GOVERNMENT

For an economic theory for the growth of government and the role played by the war, see Robert Higgs, *Crisis and Leviathan: Critical Episodes in the Growth of American Government* (New York: Oxford University Press, 1987). See also his *Transformation of the American Economy, 1865–1914; An Essay in Interpretation* (New York: Wiley and Sons, 1971). For more specific information on the wartime transformation of the economy see Leonard P. Curry, *Blueprint for Modern America: Nonmilitary Legislation of the First Civil War Congress* (Nashville, TN: Vanderbilt University Press, 1968); and for a specific application of the growth of government in the postwar period see Randy Holcombe, "Veterans' Interests and the Transition of Government Growth, 1870–1915," *Public Choice* 99 (June 1999): 311–26. Richard Franklin Bensel, *Yankee Leviathan: The Origins of Central State Authority in America, 1859–1877* (New York: Cambridge University Press, 1990), is also a classic work in this area.

INDEX

Aaron, Daniel, 85
Abolitionists, 17
Acadia (steamship), 38
Adams, John, 3
Alcoholic beverages, 51–52
American Revolution, 93
Anaconda Plan, 29, 30
Anderson, Gary, 54
Antebellum period: banking in,
    62–63; increases in productiv-
    ity, 8; industrial revolution in,
    91; labor in, 93–95; rapid
    growth and economic develop-
    ment, 61; tariffs, 19–23; wage
    growth, 8–9
Antietam, Battle of, 70
Anti-Federalists, 3
Antislavery Democrats, 4, 6, 25
Austrian School, of economics, 70

Balanced budget, federal, 12
Bank failures, 76–77
Banking: before Civil War, 60–65;
    free banking, 61, 62–63, 64, 76,
    77, 89; fundamental change in
    as result of Civil War, 76–79,
    89; wildcat banks, 63, 65, 70.
    See also National banking
    system; State-chartered
    banking
Bastiat, Frédéric, 82–83, 86
Baum, Frank, *Wizard of Oz* as
    allegory, 77–78
Beard, Charles, 2, 84
Beard, Mary, 2, 84
Bensel, Richard, *Yankee Levia-
    than*, 100

Blacks: fixed-share tenancy
    contracts for farmers, 97;
    income increases from Civil
    War to 1900, 98; population
    growth, 7; postwar decline in
    fertility and mortality, 95;
    postwar labor participation
    rates, 96–97; postwar land
    ownership, 97; and Recon-
    struction, 95–98; and skilled
    labor markets, 97; and trade
    schools, 97; turn to "group
    economy," 97
Blockade. *See* Confederate
    blockade; Union blockade
Blockade-running, 30, 46, 53–55;
    in 1863 and 1864, 52; capture
    rates, 36, 37, 43; new profit
    opportunities, 29, 34; state-
    run, 49; and steam vessels, 35
Borrowing, as method of
    financing war, 66–69
"Bricks for forts," 17
Brogan, Denis, 85
Brown, Joseph Emerson, 49
Bruce, Robert, 89
Bryant, William Jennings, 76, 77
Buchanan, James, 5, 25
Bureau of Printing and Engrav-
    ing, 99
Business: developments in
    organization, 90; preferred
    access to money market, 89;
    subsidies for, 86

Calhoun, John C., 3
Calomiris, Charles, 69

117

124

INDEX

Wall Street, 90
War: borrowing as method of
financing, 66–69; burden on
economy, 65–66; financing of
Revolutionary War and War of
1812, 75; impact on tariff
enactments, 19; taxation as
method of financing, 66, 68
War of 1812, 19, 75, 93
Weiss, Thomas, 94
West Virginia, secession from
Virginia, 82
Westward movement, 17
Whig Party, 3, 5; easy money
views, 60; interest group

support for increased federal
spending, 17; preference for
inflationary national banking
system, 64; support for high
protective tariff and "free
land," 18
Whiskey, 51–52
White terrorism, 97
Wise, Stephen, 36, 48
World War II, 82

Xenophobia, 4

"Yankee ingenuity," 91
Yosemite nature reserve, 99